# SO YOU WANT TO BE A
# CINEMATOGRAPHER?

## ... LIFE BEHIND THE LENS

by
AUSTIN F. SCHMIDT

Cover Design by Kristina Zito & Austin F. Schmidt
Copyedited by Alexa Heinicke

Copyright © 2010 Austin F. Schmidt

ISBN :145632246X
EAN-13: 9781456322465

# TABLE OF CONTENTS

# FOREWARD

The following thoughts, opinions, and observations are solely those of Austin F Schmidt. Though I imagine they reflect that of other cinematographers, I'm not sure all will agree with me. Take what I say with a grain of salt. Make your own decisions and choose what's right for you. But above all, never be afraid to take risks. It seems that is when life takes a turn for the best... or the worst– face it: the path to become a professional cinematographer has no trail map lined with clichéd catch phrases.

Over the years many individuals have approached me with questions like, "How do I become a cinematographer?" "What choices will I face?" "What decisions should I make?" Inevitably, each conversation became a pep talk to instill confidence and provide tips regarding various aspects of the industry. After responding time and time again, I decided to write all this random shit down; to provide a valuable source of reference for all the inquisitive minds out there.

My path to becoming a professional cinematographer was never glamorous. No prestigious awards were won. A movie didn't propel me to overnight recognition. And I never found a shortcut to success. Honestly, I sort of fell into it, spending many sleepless nights persevering toward my goals.

So, why is my seemingly spotlight-depraved story relevant? Because most of you, like myself, will never have that glamorous entrance into the professional field of filmmaking. What seems an arduous beginning is quite normal. As you may know or will shortly realize, there is no particular way to do what we do and make a living at it. While stumbling through the early days in my career, I was faced with many decisions. I continually searched for resources that would guide me through the steps of becoming a professional cinematographer. I simply wished to reference someone that had gone through it already. Little could be found. As a result, I vowed to share my experiences with others, keeping nothing to myself. That is why this book is relevant. It is the gift of insight written to my younger self. It is the knowledge I wished to have had access to early in my career. It is the tip of my hat to those who travel down the path of a cinematographer.

Then what the hell is this book about? Whether you desire to shoot documentaries, music videos, commercials, or feature films, a young cinematographer always begins his or her career with little possibility of keeping it. It is that time period on which this book focuses. Topics range from the personal to the technical. There are tidbits for the young mind interested in motion photography to the experienced cameraperson wanting to become a cinematographer. Elements in this book are applicable to every situation, wherever you may be presently. And if understood, its application might lessen your painful and tumultuous future.

But, before turning the next page, know this: your endeavor into the craft of cinematography will leave those dearly loved drowning in its wake. Hearts will break. Relationships will be strained. Rent may be overdue for years to come, while instant noodles become a dietary sustenance. Laugh now, but you've been warned.

# THE BEGINNINGS OF

My childhood dream was to become a world-famous soccer player. The word cinematography had no place in my vocabulary for twenty-two years. My parents taught us children to play in the woods behind our house and attend church on Sundays, instead of watching the latest flick on TV. As a result, my introduction to movies was very gradual. It began with the Walt Disney classics like *Pollyanna, Snow White,* and *Davy Crockett.* Each year more "adult" movies were allowed, such as *The Sound of Music* and *The Secret of Nimh;* definitely not the type of films that aspire one to become a filmmaker. While my friends came to school talking about the latest R-rated movie, the best I could quote from was *The Sandlot.*

I grew up in Colorado where a solitary stoplight was the center of our small town. The local single screen theatre would show a new release only a few weeks before it could be rented on VHS, so I rarely attended. I did love to watch movies, but being a part of them never crossed my mind.

When college came, I moved to San Diego, California, to major in Studio Arts without any better idea on the horizon. In all honesty, the main reason for moving to San Diego was to learn how to surf. Two years passed, and while my surfing abilities vastly improved, I quickly came to realize I would never make a living in the fine arts profession.

In one particular art class, the assignment was to create an installation. I decided to make an interactive video. A single audience member would enclose their head in a box to watch the video displayed on the opposite end. The video simulated a traumatized baby's perspective while in utero during an emergency c-section. The baby is comforted by the mother for several seconds of life before closing its eyes in death. The objective of the box was to place the viewer in a dark and tightly enclosed space to personally experience the event without any distraction. It got a decent response from the class. Of course my mom cried, telling me she was so proud. I'm not sure whether it was because of my work rather just me, as that is a general requirement of being a mom. After receiving an "A" for the assignment, I thought, "Hey, that was pretty damn fun. To hell with this starving artist stuff. I want to make movies." I applied to the University of California, Los Angeles (UCLA) film school the following month, choosing that particular school because of its close proximity to surfing waves. However, that first attempt at film school was met with a non-acceptance letter.

I spent the following years studying at a community college in San Diego, getting tossed around by misinformed career counselors and traveling the world to several surf destinations. Every year I focused on getting into UCLA, but each application or phone interview resulted in a non-acceptance letter. One such interview took place in a phone booth on the western shores of Ireland. My brother and I were surfing their waves by day while working as bartenders at night. After several failed attempts to coordinate an exact calling time with the interview committee (our time zones were eight hours apart after all), we finally connected. The line was full of static and I mistakenly called one female professor a Mrs. instead of a Ms., to which she took extreme offense. Highly disheartened after being rejected yet again, I returned to the States. My father greeted me at the Denver airport with somewhat good news. I had been accepted into New York University's (NYU) Undergraduate Tisch School of the Arts to major in film production. NYU had been my safety school in case UCLA never accepted me. It was only 'somewhat' good news, because from what I knew there wasn't any surfing in Manhattan. I was 22 years old, though I specifically remember feeling very old at the time. The younger NYU students attending since freshman year intimidated me with their knowledge during my first technical film class. So much so that I considered dropping out.

I heard rumors that cinematography was comparable to painting. Since that was all I had studied at that point, it seemed like an obvious path to pursue. The desire to be a cinematographer soon became my identity, though I had only a vague idea of what a cinematographer did, much less knew they were also called a DP (Director of Photography).

"What are you wanting to do?"

"I'm here to be a cinematographer."

"Oh, you want to be a DP, that's nice."

"No, I said I wanted to be a cinematographer."

"They're the same thing, dumb ass."

Credibility with classroom peers was lost learning that new bit of information.

# A CINEMATOGRAPHER IS...

What is a cinematographer exactly? I often find myself trying to answer this question during any type of social gathering.

"So what do you do for a living?"

"Well, I'm a cinematographer."

"Oh! What is that?"

"It's a director of photography... I shoot films for a living."

"Oh yeah, so you make films. You mean like Steven Spielberg."

"No, not exactly. He's a director. Actually it has nothing to do with directing the film."
(*Awkward moment*)

"... So what do you do then?"

"Well, I create how the film is photographed."

(*A sudden moment of apparent understanding*)
"So you are the director!

"No, no, I am responsible for the lighting, technical crew, camera movement..."

(*Frustrated and confused*)
"So you press play on the camera?"

"Well, this isn't going anywhere. I'm going to get a Heineken. It's been fun, let's do this again sometime."

And so the discussion ends, beer being more enticing than occupation explanation. To clarify the job of a cinematographer is difficult because the job parameters change from production to production. Past American Society of Cinematographers (ASC) president Richard P. Crudo wrote an article defining what we do. He did a pretty good job, so I included parts of it here.

*We are artist/scientists, with the emphasis on "artist."* Certainly, every ASC member is a master technician who can handle *any* type of production. Given that equipment predominantly characterizes the surface of our profession, it's easy to see how someone might be fooled into thinking that techno-lust is all we have to offer. But it's only through command of technique that we're able to create more than the simplest recording of what's in front of the lens.

What we do is more about the *application of taste* then anything else, and that comes from the heart. This means we are not interchangeable. The classic defense of this position always holds true: if you ask 100 cinematographers to shoot the same scene, you'll get 100 different results, and each will be valid. You may prefer one version to another, but that's more a function of how you perceive *the way we used our tools* than anything else.

*Our real job is to get inside the head of a director and render his or her vision of the story in concrete terms.* Cinematographers turn thoughts, ideas and emotions into something physically palpable. We do this by embracing *collaboration* with our directors, not by unilaterally imposing our view. Under the best of circumstances, this creative relationship starts in prep and continues through the end of post.

*Our primary tools are light, composition, movement, and supervision of the final look in the lab or digital-mastering suite, and our efforts are in the service of what we feel is appropriate of the material.* Though the director's role is often compared to that of an orchestra conductor, only one set of eyes can guide the look of a film from start to finish. With all of the new tools available these days, it has never been more important for cinematographers to protect the integrity of the original intent that we determined with the director.

*We're also managers.* It's imperative that cinematographers manipulate the "money + time + equipment + manpower" equation to our best advantage. Regardless of the budget and schedule, the challenges we face are pretty much the same every time out. Consequently, the quality of our photography is affected by every decision we make. Clearly, it's in our interest to work *with* the production to solve *any* problem[1].

The previous statement covers all the elements describing a cinematographer's job. But don't quote Mr. Crudo at a party, otherwise I guarantee you won't get laid that night.

This topic brings to mind a certain film evaluation professor. He would feverishly circle the room like a vulture; his harsh and winded critiques of a classmate's film forced many a tear. Though I disagreed with most every opinion and critique, I did respect his dedication to and passion for the craft. It was during one of his long sermons when I heard the simplest explanation of all. "We are guardians of the image," he bellowed, fist in hand.

Making a film requires many individuals, each with unique influence on the final story. It is the cinematographer's job to protect each individual's input, molding a cohesive visual product derived from the director's overall vision. However, I will place a warning label on this box. Some might confuse "guarding the image" with fighting those who may destroy it. This misinterpretation would defeat the nature of the collaborative effort. Though a cinematographer often has the most experience on a film set, do not perceive this as a right to bully others into your subjective opinion. The best cinematographers are those willing to listen, absorbing everyone and everything around them.

---

[1] Crudo, Richard. "President's Desk" <u>American Cinematographer</u> Magazine 86 Sept. 2005: 10. (Used with permission)

# FILM SCHOOL vs. THE LADDER

Superman vs. Spiderman? Mayonnaise vs. Miracle Whip? My dad vs. your dad? Film School vs. the Ladder? In the end, which of these is better? No answer has been conclusively supported in any case. There will never be one. It is too subjective, which I will explain. But first...

## – A LITTLE HISTORY LESSON –

In the early days of Hollywood, a cinematographer had to ascend what I will refer to as the "Ladder". Individuals worked up ranks within their prospective departments at a particular studio. Mentorship was the basic idea, where an individual gained first-hand knowledge of each duty and the duty of those above on the Ladder. Over the decades, this merit-based system has gradually disintegrated. The big Hollywood studios began to lose their monopoly on film production as independent films found success. Television became a demanding source for commercials, and later on, music videos. This turn in events created a sudden increase in the need for more cinematographers.

A handful of universities had been offering film courses dating back to the 1920's. They were never taken seriously, offering very little to their students in the ways of practical film production. It wasn't until the 1970's when young directors Steven Spielberg, Francis Ford Coppola, and George Lucas, fresh from Film School, created huge blockbuster hits such as *Jaws*, *The Godfather*, and *Star Wars* that Film Schools became recognized as a viable educational experience. Many students sought after the advertised "instant" success brought on by such an education. Universities scrambled to offer these types of courses, as they saw huge monetary potential from a demanding public. Despite the ever-increasing possibilities opened by the expanding field of modern media, job opportunities have remained competitive as a result of universities churning out large numbers of scholastic "cinematographers". The scales of supply and demand have never really tipped in our favor.

# – THE LADDER –

When working up the Ladder, first-hand knowledge in film production is obtained from seasoned professionals. Years are spent learning every minute detail, to impress consistency into the brain until it is second-nature. Many respected cinematographers have worked under their peers as crewmembers. What better way to learn the craft than by observing those who treaded the paths before you?

Though many possibilities exist, one of these two can be chosen to become a cinematographer; walk the path of the cameraman, or the path of the electrician. Neither is better than the other, so you should choose which one suits your particular strengths, as both departments demand different abilities.

Mind you, the thoughts expressed on the following pages are generalities. Demands and expectations change from show to show.

## The Camera Department

1. Patience – Work days can be long and boring as you wait for extravagant lighting set-ups or extended actor blocking. But, when called upon, you must be at the top of your game. Oftentimes the impossible is expected, pulling focus at low f/stops or operating the camera to find perfect frames with little to no rehearsals. Directors and producers rarely have patience for the camera department. When mistakes are made, those lowest on the food chain will generally take the fall, sometimes heavily reprimanded or even fired.

2. Acute Memory and Motor Skills – Details must be completed meticulously. Each shot must be noted and recorded in a consistent manner. Mathematical and technical information must be obtained at a moment's notice.

3. Finesse – The camera department must be able to "feel" a shot and find the right moment to execute the job. You are always closest to the actors on set while the actors are in their "mode", so respect and maturity is a must. Never be seen and never be heard is your motto, though you are expected to perform a multitude of tasks before each shot.

4. Repetition – Creating a sense of repetition within your daily routine is the key to success. This allows you to move quickly and precisely out of habit, rather than wasting time. Working in a consistent order will lessen the chance of forgetting steps or making mistakes.

5. Thick Skin – Above all, have thick skin. The camera department is a stressful arena to work in. You are responsible for the most precious item on a movie production, the film stock. If anything is ruined as a result of moisture warping, mistimed shutters, camera scratches, accidental flashing or anything else, you take the full blame. You are not expected to pay production back for the cost of ruined film, but I assure they will never hire you again. A friend once told me, "Flashing film is kind of like motorcycling. It's not a matter of if you fall down, it's a matter of when." If you make a mistake, don't try and hide it. Covering up your mistake may result in a greater loss for production and cost a lot of additional money. Imagine the trouble you'd be in if production had shot a huge car

crash scene on a roll which you had accidentally flashed but were too scared to tell anyone.

General steps to climb up the Ladder in the camera department are:

Film Loader – Your main duty is to change film camera magazines in a black bag or sealed dark room all day. You keep track of the film stock and an exact log as to where film is going, how much has been shot and how much is left, as well as notify production when stock needs to be re-ordered. Additional responsibilities include ordering camera expendables, documenting camera equipment that is shipped to and from rental houses, and organizing the camera truck.

2$^{nd}$ Assistant Camera (AC) – You must be familiar with all camera systems and their technical accessories. You are the go-between for the loader and the 1$^{st}$ AC. You aid the 1$^{st}$ AC in building the camera and changing equipment based on shot requirements. According to the 1$^{st}$ AC's wishes, you place "T" marks for the actors to find their positions. You are responsible for recording information on the clapping slate and "slating" for every camera take. A nervous moment occurs before each take, when you must call off the slate and clap the sticks. The set is completely silent and all attention is focused on you. One little slip-up in "slating" terminology leads to a barrage of verbal expletives from the director or assistant director (AD), and an embarrassing eye roll from the cinematographer. As if that isn't enough, you must record the technical specifications of each shot such as the focal length, the f/stop, the filters used etc.

1$^{st}$ Assistant Camera – You must never leave the camera, at least no further than an arms-length away. You are responsible for any physical goings-on with the equipment, whether it is changing accessories, switching filters, threading the film magazine onto the camera, dialing the f/stop, and pulling focus. This job requires a deft eye to instantly recognize an object's distance from the camera. Being talented in focus pulling makes you a highly sought-after commodity, especially if you don't need to create "focus marks" and can pull focus by eye. Nothing is more disheartening to a crew than when take after take must be repeated because focus was off. This is an extremely stressful job, as the image's focus rests solely on you and a "soft shot today can get you fired tomorrow".

Camera Operator – This is the final step on the Ladder before possibly elevating to cinematographer. The camera operator literally operates the camera. You are moving the camera with any of the multitude of camera support systems, such as geared heads, remote heads, fluid heads, or steadicam. You are responsible for physically executing any camera movement the director and cinematographer need to photograph the story. This position is a true art form. Split-second judgment calls must be made based on experience and intuition, as everything in frame rarely happens exactly the way it should. Sometimes, the cinematographer also acts as the camera operator. It depends on the cinematographer's preference as well as Union rules.

These responsibilities are the general guideline to most Union productions; however, with independent and low-budget films, these responsibilities are shared depending on the amount of people in the camera crew.

## The Electric Department

1. Physical Stamina – This job requires a lot of heavy lifting from the ground to above your shoulders. Anyone with back problems need not apply. Day in and night out, you work with heavy cabling and load large lighting equipment. Don't be fooled however, his job is filled by male and female, burly and skinny alike. Though this job does require physical prowess, the key is to work smart and safe, not show off how many cables you can string over your shoulder.

2. Patience – A coined phrase over the decades of film production has been, "Hurry up and wait". Never is this more true than for the electric department. You are expected to do an exhaustible amount of work in a fraction of the time it should be done in. However, when successful, most of production is rarely ready with you. This is always the position to be in, because if the electric department isn't ready, your head is first on the chopping block.

3. Thick Skin – Like the camera department, you must have a thick skin. Filmmaking creates stress, and that stress trickles down the ranks until someone finally lets it go. Never take it personally. Let it roll off your back and continue to do the job to the best of your ability. Remember, there's no crying in baseball! Get it... Tom Hanks in *A League Of Their Own*. No?... Okay then, moving on.

4. Repetition – Again, like the camera department, create a sense of rhythm and repetition. Doing things out of good habit will provide a more safe and secure environment. Consistency is the key to a fast and efficient working crew.

General steps to climbing the Ladder in the electric department are:

Electrics – You are a grunt that handles lights, lays cable, runs extensions, wires practicals, places the units, focus/spots them and applies any gel or diffusion to the light itself. This position is your introductory boot camp into the electrical world of equipment and protocol.

Electrical Best Boy – You are responsible for the daily command of the electrical crew. You are the electric department's representative that will communicate with the other production departments and deal directly with the film's Unit Production Manager. You are in charge of the hiring and firing of crew, work scheduling, equipment orders, equipment maintenance, expendables, safety, loading the electric trucks, and planning the layout of the power run as well as the distribution.

Gaffer – You are the cinematographer's right-hand man and will facilitate the lighting plan. You must know information about all types of equipment in order to create lighting schemes and effects. You should be efficient and fast to keep the production on time. Imagination is a key trait. Always have the ability to offer multiple options to the cinematographer. Attention to detail is important, as a gaffer's keen eye should detect hot spots, overall ambience, contrast, color temperatures and anything else that has been overlooked.

Unfortunately, working up the Ladder does not provide a guarantee. Oftentimes an individual may reach the top tier of his or her respective department, then struggle to forge that next step to cinematographer. A few reasons exist for this unfortunate situation.

If you do your job well and are highly respected as a camera operator or gaffer, that is what most people will know you as. In short, professional typecasting. Some may work their way into the Union, and quickly earn more money than ever before. They financially commit to cars, houses, children etc., and over the years become too comfortable in this lifestyle. Ultimately, they find discontentment in their job because they are unable to reach the cinematographer level. Financially, they can't take a step backward in pay scale and are stuck from their own undoing.

# – FILM SCHOOL –

From the first day of class as an NYU undergrad, I attacked this new world of beauty, individualism, and technicalities. I read everything I could get my hands on, often months before taking the actual classes. All energy and countless weeks were focused on shooting as many student films as possible.

One idea of utmost importance to keep in mind: immerse yourself in the experience completely. Film School is about learning how to educate yourself. You make the Film School; it does not make you. Shoot as many student productions as you can. It was always a competition between my peers as to who could shoot the most projects each semester. Film School provides immediate hands-on experience in the craft. But it is up to you how serious and committed to be. Students respect those with less knowledge but a good work ethic over those with haughty arrogance as a result of their experience.

Work in as many capacities as possible. Learn what is required of other positions as well. Filmmaking is a collaborative effort, but how can any work get done if no one knows what each other does? Work with as many people possible. Your first jobs will often come from relationships formed in Film School.

During the first year at NYU, I began applying to outside jobs. I knew I couldn't work on them, with school consuming all of my time; however, the intention was to practice presenting myself in interviews. I molded my pitch according to what worked best and additionally, people began to see my reel. Because I spent those school years baby stepping into the work industry, it positioned me for a larger leap once I had graduated. Many classmates began their baby steps after graduation, often working for nothing while pounding the pavement to make connections. Discouraged, the majority moved on to other occupations. A little foresight will help your chances of success.

## Undergrad, Grad, or Both?

In general, Film Schools are similar in their undergraduate and graduate departments. The classes are nearly identical, all of the content is the same, and often, the professors alternate between the two. Overall, you receive the same kind of education, regardless of which one you choose. However, there is one distinct difference between them that makes all the difference. It is generally true that undergraduate classes will consist of a younger demographic, one with less commitment and drive than their older counterparts in graduate school. For undergrads, life has only begun, having just graduated from high school and moved out from underneath their parents' wings for the first time. Each day is about experiencing everything they couldn't before. Making films seems like a fun career pursuit, and a lot easier than attending law school. Plus, it's a lot more glamorous, so why not major in that? I met a student during my first year at NYU who had the most outgoing personality in the entire class. He was endearing and funny; not the most creative, but good enough. More importantly, he seemed to have command of those around him when the job needed to be done. Having worked with him on various projects over the year, I naively assumed he would succeed in his efforts to become a director. I later found out he decided not to do the "film thing" and moved to Florida to major in Physical Education. Fortunately, he realized this early on before too much was invested. From a university faculty's standpoint, undergrad students like him are a big risk. Yes, he paid his tuition like everybody else, but a university isn't solely interested in a student's money. They also want to invest their time and effort into people who will in turn succeed and generate publicity, recognition, and respect.

On the other hand, graduate students are generally older individuals who come from different walks of life with more practical experience tucked under their belts. They have tried one thing or another, and realized that filmmaking is their passion. With rent due and bills stacking up, they recognize the sacrifice and risk they are taking, and truly understand what commitment means. They become intensely dedicated to Film School and very few leave. Because of these mental differences between student bodies, a school invests more of its efforts and attention to the graduate programs. A majority of these efforts tend to materialize through their graduate students' films. Grad students often have more access to money, rental-house, and post-production grants. I have seen the total budget of a particular grad's thesis film total around $100,000; however, $60,000 of it came in the form of these grants.

What does all this mean to a student cinematographer? In Film School, it is often the directing students who pay for their films. It gives you a great opportunity to gain experience on bigger films, with advanced equipment and higher production values. All this increases the chance of success in the festival circuit, more exposure to get noticed, and better footage for your reel (for those unfamiliar with what a "reel" is, reference page 36).

A big reason for going to Film School is meeting other people and cultivating relationships. It is these early relationships that play a big part in success at the beginning of your career. A higher percentage of grad students continue to work in the film business, whereas the percentage of undergrads is a lot smaller. I'm guessing 10% of my undergrad class is still working in some form of film production. I have received maybe a total of five jobs through previous classmates since graduation; not many considering my undergrad student body was around four hundred people. In comparison, several of my peers account many of their first feature films coming from students they had met in grad school, despite their student body consisting of only thirty people.

After two years studying in Manhattan and one summer in Prague, Czech Republic, I graduated from NYU. Fellow students had no idea what they were going to do after graduating. It was hard to make a living in the New York film industry, partly because of the decline in film production after 9-11. Having just finished Film School with little to no professional experience didn't help either. I, on the other hand, dreamt of attending graduate school at the American Film Institute (AFI) conservatory. I thought it strange that none of my classmates considered grad school. It seemed an obvious route and I assumed it would be another opportunity to learn about the profession in a specialized atmosphere. I knew that a number of successful cinematographers had attended AFI, such as Janusz Kaminski, Caleb Deschanel, Robert Elswitt, Wally Pfister, Robert Richardson, and Matthew Libatique. It seemed imperative to attend AFI for success to come. I also applied to UCLA as a backup plan in case I didn't get into AFI. Again, I made it to the interview rounds at both schools.

*(Delivered in the demonstrative manner of Alice's caterpillar)*
"You want to be a cinematographer, huh. Why?"

"I have always been fascinated with movies."

"That's not WHY you want to be a cinematographer."

(*Adjusting uneasily in my seat*)
"You're right, it's because I want to tell stories."

"Uhm Hmm, but that's not WHY YOU WANT TO
BECOME A CINEMATOGRAPHER."

(*Scrambling for what I thought they wanted to hear*)
"Umm okay ... maybe because I like to make pretty
pictures?"

By each interview's end, I felt I had failed miserably because
none of my answers seemed correct. Somehow they convinced me
that I didn't know enough about myself, much less the field for
which I was applying. It would be hopeless trying to teach me about
the latter. Needless to say, I didn't get in.

Although I was making a scant living in Manhattan after
undergrad school, I desired to move to Los Angeles. That was the
"obvious" place to be if one wanted a big career in film production.
Still determined to attend UCLA or the AFI conservatory, I
applied for their grad departments the following year and made it
to the phone interview stage... again. Mind you, this was the third
time I interviewed for UCLA and the second time for AFI.

I'm assuming most of you have heard your parents' stories
of what they were doing exactly when President John F. Kennedy
died. Parents rarely remember a sibling's birthday or even an
anniversary. But it seems each remembers exactly what street they
were driving on or what flavor of ice cream they were eating when
he was assassinated. I compare my acceptance phone call from AFI
to the JFK phenomenon. Having completed a day of shooting in
Manhattan, I had just sat down in Sammy's Thai Restaurant on 6th
Avenue just below 3rd Street. A calamari appetizer and large plate of

chicken pad thai with peanuts lay before me. I also indulged in a soda that meal because I needed a little energy from the sugar. It was 4:33 in the afternoon when I got the call from the head of the cinematography department at AFI. I was in. In my mind, I had just taken the first step to beating out Robert Richardson for an Academy Award.

Which route you choose ultimately depends on your personality and previous experiences. This seemed to affect my peers a great deal. One knew she wanted to be a director from the age of three. She attended undergrad at NYU straight out high school, then moved to LA to work in the industry immediately and has since been promoted to head of production in a production company. Another went into the Navy, started a business, had a kid, then decided he wanted to make films so attended grad school at AFI, and now works as a line producer in LA. A third went to undergrad school at NYU, followed by grad school at AFI, and now works as a cinematographer in LA. These people made their decisions based on who they were and what best suited them at the time. Could they be more successful than they are now? Maybe, or perhaps not. But each has succeeded in their own right and proven that any scenario can lead to possibilities of a future in this business.

Whether you attend undergrad, grad, or both, it is vital to promote yourself while a cinematography student. There are opportunities and awards to strive for, which garner national recognition and in turn aid in securing an agent that hopefully results in more work early in your career. The most recognized one is the ASC's Heritage Award. The student submits a film, which must be approved by the head of the school's cinematography department, then judged by a panel of ASC members. The winners (each year two or three students are chosen) receive recognition, an article in American Cinematographer magazine about their film, and the honor of receiving a plaque at that year's ASC awards gala. It may not seem like a big deal, but trust me, it is. Agencies will offer representation to Heritage Award winners regardless of work quality. I have seen many examples of a winner with maybe two or three short films under his or her belt and a very small clientele base receive representation from top Hollywood agencies, while veteran cinematographers with long-standing, big-name clientele are hardly considered. Oftentimes, an agency will try to ride the quick wave of success and take a chance, hoping the young cinematographer breaks out early in his or her career. Everybody loves a winner.

Another award is the Kodak Film School competition. Winners receive national recognition, product prizes, and the opportunity to screen their movies at the Clermont-Ferrand Film Festival. There is the Budapest Cinematography Masterclass, which is a bi-annual workshop sponsored by Kodak that occurs for two weeks during the summer. A handful of students are selected from countries around the world to learn from masters in the trade. Every cinematography professor should be aware of these and other awards, so help yourself out by asking them what is out there. Many film festivals offer cinematography awards, so convince your director to submit to them. If the director doesn't want to do so, then submit the movie yourself. Try to create as much exposure as possible.

Unfortunately, winning these accolades is not a guarantee to an early successful career. I know several students who won the ASC award, attended Budapest, screened their films at Clermont-Ferrand, yet still haven't broken into the business. A certain cinematographer that attended AFI and won the Heritage Award said his flash in the pan was great, but it took another fifteen years of working, mostly on reality-TV shows, until he shot a feature film that gave him his first legitimate break.

## Which Film School Is The Best?

At present, the most prominent schools, in no particular order, are the University of California Los Angeles, New York University, the University of Southern California, the American Film Institute, Columbia University in New York City, Florida State University, the University of Texas in Austin, and Chapman University. Having worked with filmmakers who attended each of these top schools, I have found an absolute truth: all offer the same basic immersion into the filmmaking process. The differences lie in the structure of their school system. Before choosing a Film School, I recommend reading the book "Film School Confidential". It provides great detail on well-known Film Schools around the country.

NYU focuses on independent filmmaking from the ground up. Film theory is taught along with practical techniques to apply those theories. You learn about the roles in production and are given many opportunities to practice on set. As a cinematography student, you work with film on many of the shoots. At NYU, there were twenty cinematography students with whom I "competed" to be chosen by directors. Considering that eighty films were made every two semesters, that's a lot of films you can be involved in. NYU's system allows the hungriest students to thrive. On the first day of every production class, I dropped in to screen my newest reel. I then pitched my capabilities, encouraging students to give me a chance. This created recognition around the school, along with practice for real world interviews.

AFI operates in the manner of a production studio. Their meticulous process follows strict guidelines, to which each student must adhere. The program accepts twenty students into specific areas of study: cinematography, directing, producing, editing, and production design. A regimented schedule is implemented the first year. Every student must continuously attend classes in film theory. Additional classes for the cinematography students include one technical, one theoretical, and one evaluation of each student's movie. By the end of year one, every student has four opportunities to practice in the form of three digital shorts and one film project. Any remaining time is spent crewing on classmates' shoots. The second year is less controlled and dedicated to creating a single thesis short along with another film project. Each member of the production crew raises money for the thesis movie. You only have the option to shoot on film pending school faculty approval and the amount of money the group raises. After attending AFI for two years, cinematography students graduate with four short films and two film projects. It is rare to shoot more because of the even amount of directors and cinematographers who are accepted into the program. Each receive a turn. I wasn't happy with this, as it dispelled any sense of competition. It creates a false sense of "fairness" without mentally prepping students for the hard-knock world soon to come.

Before choosing a school, evaluate its access to equipment and the opportunities offered to practice. If the school doesn't meet your needs, then there is no point in giving them your money. You may as well find a professional set, work up the Ladder, and get paid instead of paying out.

## Does Having A Film Degree Better Your Chances?

Absolutely not. I have never been asked if I had a film degree, nor has a degree in film gotten me a job. A few interviews occurred where a potential director had also graduated from a school I attended, which instilled a sense of camaraderie during the meeting but this didn't ultimately get me the job because of it. On the flip side, I have been denied a job because of a school I attended. Go figure. This particular case regarded a student's thesis from another Film School in New York. They made a point of informing me that the interview was over because they hated working with NYU students, assuming I was like all the others. Chalk it up to a little school rivalry.

### Will You Learn More At An Expensive Film School?

Not at all. As I said earlier, many of the schools offer the same information. Tuition costs rarely change that. NYU, AFI and USC are the most expensive schools at the moment. A downside to Film School is the amount of money it costs, regardless of which school you attend. Tuition continues to rise. And there is no guarantee of a solid job once you graduate. I have been paying my tuition loans for seven years and expect to do so for another ten. However, I am paying them back with money earned from the knowledge I gained in school.

### Does It Matter Where You Start?

That is an important consideration. New York approaches filmmaking with a guerrilla mindset. Each work-day is over twelve hours long. There is rarely a ten-hour turn-around between taillights (when the day's work is done) and tomorrow's call time (when you are expected on set). People are willing to work for free in exchange for experience and contacts. Everybody multi-tasks, doing whatever needs to be done regardless of their assigned role. A grip will work with electrical items and an electric will work with grip items. Compare this to a Los Angeles scene that is very studio-based. Crewmembers operate on twelve-hour days and require a ten-hour turn around. If work is needed beyond that, crew is compensated with overtime pay. Very few are willing to work for free. Many students fresh out of Film School expect to get paid. Roles are very specific and no one works outside of his or her department. A grip will put the light stand down and a sand bag on the light stand, then the electric will put the light on the stand and run power to it. These differences exist as a result of the larger film Union presence in LA. Out west, students talk about getting into the Union as the next big step in their career. Ask people in New York, and their only reference to Union is the Train Station on 14th Street.

Each filmmaking method offers its own unique advantage. The independent guerilla method forces one to improvise and think outside the box. That is when creative limits are stretched and a new kind of beauty surfaces. There are rarely enough people to do the job. Each person bends over backwards to make sure it gets done, thus creating a greater sense of pride and ownership. A tougher mental attitude and resilience to the stresses of filmmaking is formed. Alternatively, the studio system allows you to work in an organized and structured manner. This is very beneficial when dealing with huge sets and loads of equipment. It protects the individual worker so they aren't physically and mentally abused on a daily basis.

I found it valuable to learn methods in both cities. This broadened my palette of techniques and ability to solve a single problem in a multitude of ways. Los Angeles cinematographers tend to light big, using huge units backed far away that shoot through windows with few film lights used inside a room. LA has a lot of space and not many buildings go above two stories, so this approach works very well. In New York, there is very little space and streets are busy and narrow. Locations range from ground level to hundreds of floors up. Without a huge budget, it is impossible to light with big units outside the windows. Instead, smaller lights are utilized and hidden in nooks and crannies. It is difficult to quickly learn both techniques for lighting a room and requires time and practice like everything else. Attending schools on both coasts allowed me to do so.

Working in multiple cities creates relationships with crew, rental houses, and post-production facilities. This facilitates my work no matter where production is taking place, which in turn entices producers to hire me. Time and time again, producers have been impressed with how I work from home in LA and in a matter of minutes hire crew, submit equipment lists, and guesstimate location issues for a NY shoot. For me, it simply requires a few phone calls to the same people I have previously worked with in NY, remained faithful to, and maintained those connections despite the distance.

Ultimately it depends on where you want to start your career. While in school, your cultivated friendships, relationships, and connections are vital to survival as a young cinematographer. Gaining these through some school in Missisippi or Indiana doesn't help if you plan on moving to Los Angeles once school is done. You would have to completely start over. I'm not saying it isn't doable, it just makes it increasingly difficult and the process will probably take longer.

# – CONCLUSION –

Sorry, there is none. Basically, it boils down to different schools of thought. The Ladder allows an individual to learn from professionals on set, yet offers little hands-on experience as the cinematographer. Film School requires one to discover filmmaking independently, and offers students hands-on experience. Neither is a shortcut, nor guarantees a future behind the lens.

I do not want to create the misconception that you must choose one over the other. Many cinematographers have done both. After completing Film School, either undergrad or grad, they joined the on-set ranks as a crewmember. Think of it as a continuation of education. This approach allows you to apply technical knowledge and work ethic obtained in Film School in a professional film atmosphere. At the same time, watch and learn from those more experienced around you. This is a great way to make a living, as your early cinematography career probably won't pay enough.

There is an important time, though, when you must say, "I am a cinematographer," and decline other jobs. Whatever position you are filling to make ends meet is how people recognize you. They never see you as something else. Daryn Okada, ASC, told me of his early career and steps that led to his working as a cinematographer. He never attended Film School but began working on student films in every position. Over time, he was pushed into the role of gaffer because people noticed his ability and interest in lighting. Once in a while he was asked to shoot, but never enough to commit full-time. He finally decided, "That's it, I don't work in that position. I'm not a gaffer anymore, I'm a cinematographer." Work didn't pour in right away; however, those around viewed him in a different light.

He made less money in the beginning, but slowly jobs in that capacity increased and so did the pay.

The idea of Film School vs. the Ladder has been a bone of contention within the cinematography world for quite some time. I was curious what percentage of ASC members were school kids or climbers. A list was compiled with this distinction in mind. After months of digging, the results were not conclusive because of incomplete historical information on all the current members. An inquiry to the ASC President was made, though it resulted in very little information. His response stressed that the ASC "is not concerned about these things to keep any records."

From the records I did compile, it was evenly split: the majority of newer members attended Film School and older members worked up the Ladder. This is a direct reflection of film production history that introduced this chapter. Although the ASC is split, the current trend reveals that Film School has helped the newer flock of members in one form or another. Since the older members (including the ones I couldn't find info on) were of the Ladder generation, I foresee the scales tipping in favor of school kids over the next decade. On a side note, some of those school kids did work up the Ladder in one way or another after attending a Film School. Another interesting fact is that the majority of ASC members, old and new alike, pursued higher education in one of any number of fields prior to becoming a cinematographer.

## Self-Education

Educating yourself should never end. There are numerous cinematography books on topics ranging from the technical to the philosophical. Several I would recommend are:

*Masters of Light* – by Dennis Schaefer and Larry Salvato: A compilation of interviews with several famous and influential cinematographers such as Conrad Hall, Haskell Wexler, Gordon Willis and Owen Roizman. Each cinematographer offers detailed insight about his career path, philosophy and technical approach to specific films.

*Cinematography: Theory and Practice* – by Blain Brown: The title is self-explanatory. Brown skillfully addresses theoretical practices when visually telling a story. He also speaks on the technology used to tell that story such as optics, light, photochemical processes, and equipment. This book has been my bible.

*Practical Cinematography* – by Paul Wheeler: Similar to Brown's yet different, as Wheeler is a British cinematographer and his take on specific topics is sometimes different. This exemplifies how our craft is based on personal preference and experience rather than technical data.

*Every Frame a Rembrandt* – by Andrew Laszlo, ASC: Laszlo relives five different productions from his career, recounting the process of each from pre-production to post.

*Reflections: Twenty-One Cinematographers at Work* – by Benjamin Bergery: Provides detailed techniques in the form of illustrations, diagrams, still frame reproductions and knowledge of twenty of the most honored cinematographers. This is a personal favorite and must-read for any aspiring student.

*New Cinematographers* – by Alex Ballinger: Contains extended studies of six young major cinematographers in today's Hollywood system. The book evaluates each cinematographer's films, up to the book's current publication date.

Periodicals are also a great source for information, such as the American Cinematographer Magazine and the International Cinematographers Guild Magazine. They contain interviews with cinematographers discussing techniques used in current movies. In pre-production, directors often like to communicate using other films as an example. These magazines are useful to learn what was done before and how you might manipulate specific approaches for your current needs.

The Internet is full of informative websites and newsletters created by cinematographers for cinematographers. Most have dialogue forums, such as www.cinematography.com, that allow individuals to post questions and responses based on their experiences. The Cinematography Mailing List, or CML, connects your email directly to their forum, allowing for instant updates on topic discussions. When reading forums on the Internet, never assume anything to be absolute fact, especially in the world of cinematography. Because of the variables in this craft, one person's opinion and approach might not work for another. In fact, people are often incorrect with the information they provide. While websites and forums are a great place to begin your search to narrow down questions, always research and do your own tests. Personal experience is irreplaceable.

Working up the Ladder isn't the only way to educate yourself on a professional set. Some cinematographers allow individuals to "shadow" them while working. Shadowing means exactly what it sounds like: observing a cinematographer without intruding on their ability to work. Contact the cinematographer directly and if unsuccessful, approach through his or her agent. A

personal letter should be written explaining your desire to shadow
them. More often than not, a response will never be received, but
occasionally a few are delighted to offer a visit to their set. Each
opportunity can be eye-opening. The most interesting aspect is to
see these cinematographers face locations and situations similar to
those that you do; but how they choose to light these situations sets
each one apart. One can also observe how the crew is run and how
communication is passed down the ranks of electrics and grips.
Some cinematographers speak very little, if at all. A simple word
and entire universes shift in unison. Others are animated, barking
orders and motioning to the closest person nearby. The way a set
operates is a direct reflection of the cinematographer's personality
and can often set the tone of the entire set.

# LIFE AFTER COMMITMENT

Many decisions are faced along the path to becoming a professional cinematographer. Most pertain to you as an individual and the presentation of yourself to the world. From conference call interviews to visual presentations, nothing should ever be taken lightly. You may only get one chance to impress.

# – REELS –

A reel is the way a young cinematographer attains work. It is an assembly of footage from previous films you have created; a visual resume if you will. Once recognition is attained, the need for a reel lessens.

Before compiling your reel, I recommend first looking at those of other professional cinematographers. Most agencies make their clients' reels available online for anyone to view. Observe as many as possible. You will notice that each cinematographer differs in his or her presentation, as it directly reflects each individual self. Take this into account. No matter how you choose to showcase yourself, always make it "you".

## What Should My Reel Consist Of?

Though industry standards do exist, I have found client preferences differ from coast to coast and person to person. You won't be able to please everyone. Instead, choose images that best represent your abilities and range. Quality is far more important than quantity. Directors fixate on poor footage, forgetting all the beautiful shots. Before finalizing your reel, ask someone impartial to watch it. We tend to fall in love with elements of our own work, remembering what it took to capture it. Just because a shot is technically challenging doesn't mean it showcases our ability. It is important to have another objective opinion weigh in.

## How Should My Reel Be Presented?

Presentation depends on the type of work you want and who you are appealing to. Some narrative reels are displayed in a montage format with one or more pieces of music underlying the imagery. The montage consists of random footage taken from multiple movies intending to show the cinematographer's range of capabilities. It allows the client to see more examples in a short amount of time. Not all people agree with this approach, as only the "pretty" shots are shown. A cinematographer is responsible for visually telling an entire movie, not just specific shots, so some believe a reel should consist of scenes from several productions shown in their entirety. These scenes often include the dialogue and sound design from the movie as well. This approach allows the client to accurately see how a cinematographer visually tells a story. Do not show a scene with two similar shots; two people conversing at a table, for example. This won't effectively showcase your range and quickly becomes boring to watch.

Think about who you are trying to impress. Clients will sit for only so long before ceasing to be interested. Most have made up their mind whether to consider you in the first minute. For this reason, I recommend containing your reel to five minutes. If they want to see more, they will ask for additional examples and you know at this point that you've captured their interest.

Music video and commercial reels are different because each individual piece is less than five minutes long. A commercial or music video reel contains several examples that the potential client can view in their entirety. Too few examples, and the client assumes you have little experience. Too many means everything you ever did is on there. Again, five seems to be the magic number.

## — SELF-PROMOTION —

Three years ago, self-promotion required submitting DVD copies to hundreds of potential clients via snail mail. Not only was stock and postage costly, but by the time a client received the material the position might have already been filled. In this age of instant gratification, a young cinematographer mailing out hard copies will soon be an old cinematographer solely supporting the United States Postal Service.

The Internet is a more common way to reach potential clients, with its instant accessibility. Use it to your advantage in the form of a personal website. I'm not talking about a site with some still images and a photo of yourself next to a film camera. It should be a professionally designed and interactive website, where a potential client can learn about your services in an effortless manner and access a quality reel quickly. Having created a website several months before graduating film school, interest in my work jumped rapidly. People continually called because my site "was so impressive that they knew I must be a great cinematographer". On several occasions, inquiries were made without having even seen my reel, basing it solely on the website. Whether through personal websites, business cards, emails, flyers or reels, remember that you specialize in the visual medium. Make everything representing you reflect that.

Once a website is complete, locate Internet listings to advertise your services. Some Internet listings are free, such as www.mandy.com, but others like LA 411 or NY 411 require a fee. With any listing, there is an easy way to create an advantage. Not everyone can relate to this; however, those who felt discriminated against at a younger age will appreciate my correlation. Remember those days in elementary school, when everyone lined up according to their last names? Whether for the drinking fountain, Wednesday cupcake day, or lunchtime potty breaks, those whose last names came later in the alphabet were always at the end of the line. Such is the way of Internet service listings. With a last name like Schmidt, clients have to scan page after page to finally stumble upon my listing. Clearly they will find a capable person long before reaching the "S" names. For those who suffer from last names located toward the end of the alphabet, create a unique name listing to get placed on an earlier page. I entered my first name as Schmidt and my last name as Austin, which landed me a location on the first page in the A's. Calls increased immediately thereafter.

## — PLATFORMS FOR PRACTICE —

You must constantly create opportunities to hone technical skills and work with every type of person possible. This can be accomplished by shooting student films. Locate the film schools in your area. Create an advertisement flyer announcing yourself and provide contact info. Make sure it pops out against other nearby flyers. Next step, place it on every bulletin board in the schools for students to discover you. Every few months, revisit the boards to refresh them with new flyers. Contact the school administration and ask to attend the first production classes of each semester, so you can screen your reel and "pitch" yourself to the students. These student films are perfect opportunities to work on your craft, receive fodder for your reel and gain relationships that may result in work after these students are out of school.

There are different avenues for practice if you are pursuing a career as a music video or commercial cinematographer. Initially, the budget comes out of the director's and/or cinematographer's pocket. Invest just enough to make your work look professional. Do not cut corners that affect the quality. You are breaking into an industry that is teaming with professional people; anything less and potential employers will quickly move on to the next person. The goal is to make your work look like that seen on TV. The key is to create visuals that are unique and stunning; that stand out and introduce you as an asset that can't be found elsewhere. Research commercial and music video production houses to find which ones do not have other cinematographers with your particular style. Once you have three to five quality pieces assembled into a reel, begin delivering the assembly to your selected production houses. Ask to meet the production head personally. A production house receives multitudes of reels every day, so footage is screened by interns working for free or school credit. Meeting the department head allows for personal introduction and places your face together with the work. This approach does not make your work any better, if it lacks then it lacks, but it helps you stand out from the crowd. Another approach to get your foot in a production house door is to directly work for them. Even if that means interning for free. While shooting on your free time, work in the company to form relationships that give direct insight and access to these very tight-knit people. They prefer to hire from within, so your outside work will be reviewed and critiqued more seriously.

When becoming a commercial cinematographer, you begin working on spec commercials. These are not official commercial spots; rather, mock-ups using real products. Do not worry about copyright issues, as the purpose is to show a production house your ability to sell a product, not to make actual money. A spec should be 15 or 30 seconds long (the standard television running times). Commercials are the best way for a cinematographer to experiment and take risks. Each shot must stand out and highlight your abilities. You only have thirty seconds to impress the audience. Make each frame count.

Loving music is a must for a music video cinematographer. If the love for music isn't there, how do you expect to express its emotions visually? Attaining the opportunity to express those emotions is another matter entirely. Approach independent bands that want a music video. Like spec commercials, funds will generally have to come from your pocket. On occasion, the band may be able to pitch in, but these starving artists typically have less money than you do. Attend live shows, introduce yourself to the managers, do what you can to gain a personal contact with them. For musicians, artistic decisions are made from personal opinions and are not business-oriented. They would rather hire a friend who is less talented than someone unfamiliar despite their obvious talent.

When a week or two goes by with no work, I get anxious and invent schemes to limit my days of no work in the future. One such scheme hatched after a weekend of helping my brother shoot a school film project down in Mexico. The footage turned out beautiful, honest, and unique. We cut the images to a particular musician's pre-release single before his album came out. The plan was to introduce a visual proposal to wet the musician's appetite for our eventual music video pitch. We were nobodies without a professional track record, so proving our ability might convince them to work with us. I contacted Iron & Wine's manager and was given permission to send it directly to them. One week later, the manager informed us they had just completed a video for the song; however, he liked what we did better than the studio-approved version. Disappointed but not disheartened, we continued to cut the footage to pre-release songs until someone hired us. I had not heard of this approach before, but it seems like a logical way to demonstrate to musicians what you can do versus submitting a verbal proposal.

Unfortunately, music videos and television commercials are a dying form of production, as the world's media outlets and advertising strategies continue to evolve. Finding cinematography jobs in either area is increasingly more difficult. Don't pigeonhole yourself into one or the other. Developing relationships in both from the beginning gives you more to fall back on during tough times.

# — EQUIPMENT PURCHASE —

After graduating from NYU, I shuffled along bread lines with fellow classmates in New York. I tried to work as an assistant cameraman, but all I wanted to do was shoot. How could I get work doing just that and still make enough money to pay rent? People wouldn't hire me based on my student experiences. I had to offer something other young cinematographers could not; cheap camera equipment rentals. As a bonus, my cinematography "expertise" came with the equipment. This provided the extra benefit of learning how to run a camera rental business, market myself as a cinematographer, and slowly piece together a decent reel while specializing in 35mm photography. Before purchasing the camera package, I advertised myself in film schools and New York City as a 35mm cinematographer to initially stir interest. This isn't to say that the camera package created a highly profitable living. I barely made enough to pay the camera loan and living expenses, sometimes needing financial assistance from my parents. But it was a means to an end. At least I was doing what I loved and quickly gaining more experience than most peers my age.

If you choose to invest in equipment, I recommend it to be a camera. A camera owner is assumed to be a cinematographer and is treated as such by all potential employers. People believe it reflects the serious nature with which you approach the craft. A production rarely rents your camera equipment without hiring you as the cinematographer. Owning a camera package provides a distinct advantage in our highly competitive industry: cheaper rental rates. As the owner, you have the ability to charge lower rates compared to a rental house because you have little business overhead. Although we prefer to think that we as cinematographers are hired based on capability, this is generally untrue in the low-budget world where money reigns, and experience is sacrificed for the almighty dollar. As a young cinematographer with a camera package, you are hired not for YOU but for cheap equipment rental. And that's okay. It creates a distinct advantage that enables you to stand out amongst other individuals vying for the same position. It does not guarantee that you'll get the job, but certainly increases the chances. This directly affects the amount of work you gain, which in turn provides more reel footage and establishes additional relationships. My camera provided a great resource for the low-budget market and made both parties happy. Filmmakers saved costs and were able to shoot on a high-end format, while I was able to make a living and create a quality reel containing 35mm footage.

Don't assume owning equipment is easy, however, and that once the big purchase is made work will automatically flow in. There are variables to this scenario and risks to consider. It is a costly endeavor, and should not be taken lightly.

In this day and age, the digital world has become a viable source of origination. Many people believe it will eventually replace film. I have no intention of breaching that argument. Instead, I will speak from an owner's standpoint. The digital revolution continues to surprise and amaze every year. The technology advances are extremely beneficial to us as filmmakers, but not necessarily us as camera owners. Once a digital camera is released, an improved version appears on the market again in six months. Popular digital cameras used early in my career two years ago are now viewed as dinosaurs because of their short shelf-life. If you invest in one, make sure it pays for itself in a one-year time span. The continual need for upgrades to meet client demand becomes costly over the years. Alternatively, film cameras survive for decades before retirement.

The film camera I purchased was manufactured in the mid 80's and continues to be used in the industry. Like digital, film cameras are constantly updated; however, these updates involve a decrease in body weight and an increase in sophisticated electronics. These upgrades are helpful, but do not affect an older camera's ability to keep up with newer models. The quality of an image is exactly the same whether an older or newer film camera is used. Because of a film camera's stability, it pays for itself over a longer period of time.

Consider the type of cinematographer you want to become when choosing which camera to purchase. If you want to shoot documentaries, a digital camera makes sense. Digital stock is more cost-effective compared to negative and film processing prices. If becoming a commercial or music video cinematographer is your desire, then a camera with flexibility and options should be top on the list. If a narrative cinematography position is more to your liking, purchase a sturdy camera that will perform on a long-term basis with low maintenance requirements. Most importantly, choose which type of medium you want to work in, film or digital. A stereotype forms early in your career, creating a long, hard road to travel. If you purchase a digital package, you are perceived to be a digital cinematographer; if you purchase a film camera, then a film cinematographer. Unfortunately, that's just the way things are.

Before purchasing a camera, research everything about the equipment and technical side of ownership. Learn it's general maintenance and parts replacement. Every time it is brought to an equipment facility for repairs, that's an additional cost that you have to eat. I prefer cameras with few bells and whistles. The more toys a camera has, the more likely it will break down. A camera should provide the basic necessities that a production requires. For feature films, the camera must operate from 12 to 50 frames per second (fps), change its shutter angle, and provide a video feed for the director. In music videos or commercials, camera requirements are the same with increased frame per second capabilities and the ability to ramp speeds. Ramping is a technique used to alter the frame rate during a shot. It allows images to change from slow motion to fast motion or vice versa while maintaining correct exposure.

Inquire about insurance rates and business legalities. Create binding contracts to protect yourself from any mishaps. Speak with other cinematographers who own equipment to learn from their mistakes and triumphs. Most importantly, represent yourself and your work well. Naive productions assume you know what you are doing if you own professional equipment. Don't prove them wrong.

## — WORKING OUTSIDE THE BOX —

An inconvenience as a young cinematographer living in Manhattan is the winter months are extremely cold. Not only outside on the freezing streets, but also in the bare bank account. I needed something to help supplement my low income during that time of the year. I had taken the leap into the cinematography void by purchasing a camera package and publicly declaring myself a cinematographer, but I wasn't always able to pay the rent. In the beginning, most cinematography work will be done for free during sixteen-hour days and seven-day weeks. You may have to work a more stable job to supplement the measly film pay. The job must be flexible enough to take time off for shooting without getting fired in the process. Many people choose to work as a crewmember; however, I happened to stumble on another solution.

While walking in lower Manhattan a little after my 24th birthday, I passed by a film school and stepped in on the off-chance they might be looking for assistant teachers. After reviewing my resume, they offered me a teaching position. I was surprised but ecstatic, thinking this would be a piece of cake plus solve my money issues. They only required me to teach a mock class in front of several school department heads. I confidently stepped into the classroom the next day; and was asked to leave five minutes later. The technicalities of cinematography were second nature to me, but verbalizing them was something I had never done before. Very politely they expressed confidence in my knowledge, but knew I could not teach at their school's standards. They happily offered me an assistant teaching position instead. Perfect! That's what I wanted in the first place. The work schedule was flexible, allowing assistant teachers to sign up for shifts as desired. This allowed me to shoot whenever possible, and make money as an assistant teacher between shooting days.

The ensuing months were spent watching other teachers' approaches in the classroom. I was confident I knew all that they did, and instead observed how they conveyed it to others. Based on several teachers' recommendations, the department offered me a chance for redemption. I spent the next week forming a lesson plan, drawing diagrams, and rehearsing over and over. My girlfriend at the time, poor thing, bared through it all feigning interest while asking questions during my practice "lectures". The second attempt went off without a hitch and I began teaching that January. I was extremely nervous the first day. After the initial introduction and roll call was completed, I looked to the chalkboard and froze at the diagram I had drawn. What did it mean again? What was I talking about? I had no clue what I was doing or what I was going to say. After moments that seemed like hours, my mind kicked into autopilot and words stumbled out. I'm not sure what they were, but they continually came in a steady and discernable stream. The session finished and not one student raised a hand in question. It appeared everybody understood the lesson completely. Days later I discovered I was given the adult foreign class and English wasn't their first language. Bogged in a haze of bizarre technical English words, how could I expect them to apply those terms to the cinematographic process? Over the following weeks, I devised different ways to communicate with the students, spending large amounts of time after class to ensure their comprehension. This experience began to affect my professional work outside the room. I formed a greater degree of patience and the increased ability to communicate aspects of my work with producers and directors unversed in the technicalities of motion picture photography. In the end, I learned as much from them as they did from me.

# — RELATIONSHIP GAMES —

A cinematographer's success is dependent on the directors and producers with whom he or she has previously worked. As a director rises in status, the cinematographer is sometimes allowed to follow. Darrin Aronofsky attended AFI with cinematographer Matthew Libatique. When Aronofsky directed his first feature, *Pi*, Libatique was asked to lens the film. They have worked together ever since. While attending a film festival, Christopher Nolan saw a movie shot by Wally Pfister. Impressed with the imagery, he hired Pfister to shoot his next film, *Memento*. The rest is history. Unfortunately success in Hollywood is not always that straight forward. Having shot all of a director's early work does not guarantee a position on his or her first funded feature. Producers often require a first-time feature director to hire a seasoned cinematographer. This lowers the risk of their investment, as the veteran cinematographer provides a sense of stability on set and insures the financiers of a quality product. This is standard in the industry, so don't be insulted when it happens. Continue the relationship with your director. If his or her first film is a success, producers let go of the reigns and allow the proven director to hire who they want on the next movie.

Every cinematographer speaks fondly of the people they have formed relationships with in the working field. Filmmaking creates tight-knit bonds, as together we battle late working hours, freezing nights, bland food, cold coffee, and stale bagels. My career has traversed many a road, rocky and smooth, yet certain individuals stick by me. For that, I give my undying support and continually hire them. Loyalty and camaraderie is vital. Though some jobs may not pay well, you always need competent crewmembers. Respecting them from the beginning ensures their commitment, whether it's for high-paying films or low. The relationship with your crew is irreplaceable. Don't let inexperienced directors, budget-hacking producers, or unorganized assistant directors deter your respect for and appreciation of your team. Remember, you are only as good as the crew working WITH you. No one should ever work FOR you.

I was hired to shoot a narrative short with dogs running around Manhattan's Riverside Park. Many shots required fast, complicated camera work ending in perfectly composed frames. Because of budgetary constraints, I was forced to use a dolly to capture the animals' movements. Most dolly grips I had worked with needed subjects to hit their marks in order to place the camera in the perfect frame. This was of no use to me, considering the animals' inconsistent and sudden body movements. I had to find a person who could discover the frame based on his or her intuition. A certain individual I had previously worked for when he directed a short film had continually impressed me with his ability to operate the camera and find good frames at a moment's notice. Though he had never operated a dolly before, I figured teaching him dolly operation would be easier than asking dogs to hit their marks. Thinking it would be a fun experience, he showed up the morning of our first shooting day. The key grip spent thirty minutes teaching him the ropes of the Fisher 11 dolly. Half an hour after the lesson, the first shot was up and of course the dog missed his mark completely. Even worse, the camera movement and timing was horrendous. Had I made a mistake and taken too much of a risk? I looked back at the director-turned-dolly grip and said, "You know what went wrong." He nodded back. That was the last take the dolly ever presented a problem. He has since dolly-gripped with me all over the country, and I continue to photograph every production he directs. We still laugh about that shoot. The producers were never aware of the situation, ultimately praising him for such dolly "expertise".

A relationship should also be established with film stock manufacturers, equipment rental houses, and post-production facilities. It is important to be in good standing and on a first-name basis with these people, as they can directly assist any production you work on. Your first movies are always low budget and can rarely afford quality equipment or services. But if you have established a relationship with those individuals, they will more than likely want to help. You are the future of their business and they will treat you like an investment. After trying different rental houses, I chose the one I liked most and continually rented from them. A short while later, they offered me discounted rental rates. That also occurred with a post-production facility. They in turn lowered the cost of processing and hourly rate for telecine transfer. I primarily shoot Kodak instead of Fuji. This isn't to say I like one over the other; it's just that cinematographers are creatures of habit and consistency, of which I am guilty as well. I have always bought stock from the same sales agent. Over time, she lowered the price for every production. All of these savings make you more appealing to a producer. On several occasions, I was considered for the job specifically because of the savings I could provide as a result of these relationships.

Associate with as many people as possible. Take meetings, invite people for drinks, and attend festivals. You never know which contact will lead to the next job. You never know which movie will garner attention. As most things in life, it will be the one you least expect. Success as a cinematographer comes down to sheer luck. To improve your chances of winning that lotto ticket, you have to create the opportunities.

The beginning years of a cinematographer's career are very hard. Strain is put on personal relationships like never before. You find out who your true friends are. If you haven't shared your career aspirations with those around you, now is the time to do so. Explain to them what you are doing and let them know the support you need. Things you used to enjoy have to be put on the back burner for a time. On many occasions, I couldn't go out to enjoy a beer or movie with friends. Those that knew what I was going through often offered to pay. Begrudgingly I accepted their offer, vowing to one day do the same for other individuals who were in my position. Often, those you love will ask for more commitment, more effort, and more passion. "Why is this job more important than spending time with me?" Sometimes they will never understand. Being a cinematographer is a selfish act, and to achieve success, it is vital. Make sure that putting those relationships at risk is worth it. Over the years, you will learn how to juggle both personal and work. If successful, life will smooth out over time so you can return what you owe.

## – THE BEST ADVICE –

Persistence will prevail. One can become discouraged during the early times in a cinematography career. You have worked long, hard days, but seen few fruits from your labor. The next step is nowhere in sight. But, don't stop now. Perseverance wins in the end. The longer you stick it out, the less competition you will face. Most of your peers aren't able to handle the pressure and opt for stable jobs, consistent paychecks and definitive work hours.

I remember countless months when no one hired me. Bills stacked up. Everything spun wildly out of control. Then from nowhere, a job came and the world resumed its natural rotation. A particular instance comes to mind. I had gone four months without working a single day. Not because I couldn't seal the deal in interviews, there just weren't many jobs available at the time. I was down to my final month of saved money with no hint of a job on the horizon. An offer had been made to purchase my camera rig and I was afraid I might have to sell it in desperation. Late one night, I received an email from a production in England that needed specific pick-up shots. Scenes in their movie took place in Los Angeles, and although they had cheated the interiors in England, they couldn't afford traveling to LA to shoot the establishing exterior shots. The next week, we communicated through a slew of emails and settled on what needed to be done. I loaded my camera package into my brother's VW van and we putted around the city, shooting tourists on Sunset Boulevard, planes landing at LAX, and limousines driving through Beverly Hills. In those two days of work, I made enough money to allow me to survive in this crazy business for another three months without selling the camera.

# WHERE ART MEETS BUSINESS

From childhood we are encouraged to find a job in what we love. Making money isn't as important as being happy. Growing older, we realize to remain in love we must first make money. Such is the conundrum of life. Producing movies is a business first; an art form second. The cinematography profession is no different.

# – THE INTERVIEW PROCESS –

During the first few years, I cut my teeth on short films, music videos, and spec commercials. The first feature continued to elude me. My reel and website helped get to this point, but I seemed to have a hard time sealing the deal after every feature interview.

Getting work is the most important objective, regardless of the script, budget, or those involved. You cannot afford to be picky at this stage, so take every job possible. Realize this about early interviews: you are not considered because of experience or body of work; rather, because you are willing to work long days for little to no pay. And that is okay. Low-budget filmmaking is the best way to gain experience and is a natural stepping-stone to becoming a seasoned professional. For a cinematographer, these interviews are about listening and understanding the client's perspective on life, love, and their favorite flavor of ice cream. Filmmakers conducting these types of interviews love to talk about themselves and the production they are passionately involved in. Their objective is to convince you to work for as little money as possible. They are only interested in hearing exactly how you will conduct yourself, according to their pre-conceived notion of a cinematographer's role. This time period can become frustrating, as your abilities are typecast based on your fledgling reel. If they don't see what they are looking for, the assumption is that you are unable to provide it. Hence, it is important to listen throughout the interview and ask educated questions. Feel out what they are looking for.

Don't worry, interviews will not always be like this. As you mature in the profession, so do the individuals involved. Interviews focus more on your personality because the client is already aware of your abilities. These professional interviews are more for the director and producer to see if your aesthetic views meet and if your personalities will connect. In these situations, you are not the only one being interviewed; you are interviewing them as well. If it doesn't look like you can work with these individuals, don't take the job. At this level, the quality of work affects your career, and doing a job badly can hurt your reputation. During these interviews, feel free to express your opinion. Good producers and directors do not alter their decision-making because you initially see something differently than they do. They know you can technically deliver what they are looking for, so instead are most interested in your perception regarding the visual telling of their story.

Rejection followed upon rejection once I began sitting in professional interviews. Although disheartened, I formed a few simple rules to bolster the appearance of my professionalism. These rules are not tricks; rather, practical applications of common sense.

Always, always, always be early. Give yourself extra time for travel. You can never foresee problems, from car accidents, to re-routed subway lines, or inaccurate computer map directions. Being there early and waiting looks better than arriving a few minutes late. How do you expect to be taken seriously for the job if you can't show up to the first interview on time?

Dress appropriately. I'm not saying to wear a suit coat and tie; generally pants and button-down shirt will do. Do not carry a childish attitude, thinking backward hats, torn jeans, and sagging pants below your boxers look mature. You need the job more than the production needs you, so portray an attitude of confidence and respect with every handshake.

Carry extra copies of your reel. The interviewer might not have kept your mailed DVD reel on file. Give them the option to pop in a copy you brought. This will jog their memory and provide a direct connection between you and your work. It creates a basis for conversation to progress in multiple directions, allowing for discussions on previous experiences that apply to their production.

Read the script several times before sitting across from them. Nothing is more unprofessional than the inability to answer questions about the storyline because you only glanced through the script once beforehand. Being a professional begins with outward appearance, and over time works itself inward.

The key is to make yourself stand out amongst a multitude of others. Do this by creating a visual breakdown with imagery to supplement your thoughts. We do work in visual media after all. Begin by reading the script straight through to get an overall idea of the story. Read it once more for the layers beneath the story. At this time, write down thoughts on how to provide visuals to those underlying layers. The breakdown should contain ideas regarding camera techniques, character portrayals utilizing particular lighting styles, certain colors to create moods, along with visual references. The length of your notes is of no importance. Whether they agree with your ideas doesn't matter. This extra effort shows the client your level of professionalism and serious approach to their film. This groundwork encourages conversation regarding the script, setting you apart from previous interviews and above the other cinematographers. The following pages contain a visual breakdown I created. It impressed the director to such an extent he offered me the job immediately.

## — *CONSTELLATION* VISUAL BREAKDOWN —
(Names have been changed for legal reasons)

Technical Intentions:
— Frame for a 1:2.35 aspect ratio. This story is about the void and emptiness the characters inhabit. Using the 1:2.35 frame shows the suppressive emptiness of space surrounding them.

— Shoot in the Super 35mm format. This allows us to frame for a 1:2.35 aspect ratio, yet avoid various characteristics of anamorphic lenses that may complicate the technical requirements within the script. Super 35mm shoots 3-perf, which will save money in postproduction since this is going through a digital intermediate (DI). Renting a super 35mm 3-perf camera is the same price as a regular 35mm camera; however, it saves money in film stock and processing as it uses about 25% less.

— Shoot on color negative rather than black & white (B&W). Though the final look of this film is mostly B&W, there are certain sequences with color mixed in. Originating on color negative makes it easier pull color out in a DI rather than add it later. Plus the newer color films stocks lend themselves to a "cleaner" look than the old B&W.

Overall Aesthetic:
— The movie is B&W, with pointed and purposeful moments where color is introduced, i.e. tears, trumpet, and blood. We should never see the actual change of color in frame. Rather, the item is subtlety introduced in color. For example: the tear shouldn't be halfway dripping in B&W, then gradually turn blue. It should start blue

when it drips. The items should not be completely colorful. Instead, have hints of color within reflections and bright points. Reference the techniques used in *Pleasantville* before certain people were colored in all the way.

– There should be elements of noir lighting. *Dark City* came to mind while reading the script. There needs to be a balance so as not to create an unbelievable world of surrealism. Instead, a noir-reality where motivated light will be seen. Another example is a few select scenes from *Requiem for a Dream*, i.e. the conversation below the wooden boardwalk at night. Stylized, yet realistic; blend between the two previously-mentioned films. Unify the night scenes and day scenes, so it doesn't look like the night is over-lit and the day looks like a low-budget film with little influence on the world the characters are in. This can be done with quality pre-production and location scouts to assess which time of day is better for each location. Because the night will naturally have contrast, it is beneficial to match the day with similar contrast and rich blacks.

– As an overall aesthetic, we should place bright sources of light deep in the background when characters are in the outside world. The area they inhabit is a darker, depressing place reflected by their emotions; however, the world around them isn't. It shows the audience there is something else beyond the lives the characters lead. Life for everyone else isn't bad; just for the characters through their own actions. Though dark in the foreground where our characters inhabit, perhaps the bright light in the far distance shows us there is a "brighter" life to have.

– Don't be afraid of shadows or not seeing the actors' faces. Let them walk in and out of light. The silhouette of talking people is just as powerful as seeing them in full detail.

– There needs to be a balance between "realistic" characters like Shade and Samantha. At first they seem like real people, but as the story evolves, we subtlety show that perhaps they are something different, i.e. Al Pacino in *Devil's Advocate*.

– Camera movement should be approached in a classical sense. No handheld (only used for violent scenes). Purposeful camera moves should accentuate certain actions and moments of emotional and physical transition for the characters as well as the audience, i.e. *Once Upon a Time in the West*.

Character Portrayals:

Tom: Tom's mood is reflected on the area he immediately inhabits. This will be done using different qualities of light, i.e. soft, hard; the angles at which they strike a surface, i.e. high, low; and ambient light level, i.e. angrier and sad more contrast, happier and content less contrast.

Heather: Heather should be top lit. The world crushes her, pulled down by the very shadows she creates.

Samantha: Samantha walks through pools of light in the areas she inhabits, allowing people only what she wants them to see. She hides more than she reveals. Some light pools will be overexposed to create halation, a glow of beauty only to fall into the unknown darkness.

<u>Shade</u>: Constantly stepping out of deep shadows when he enters a scene. Lit in silhouette more than anybody but mostly side lit, so we only see one half of his face, leaving the other mysterious. However, we always see his eyes. They pierce whatever they gaze on. When that is the focus, the rest of him seems to fade into blackness. Photograph his scenes with tilt shift lenses. These provide a different perspective of focus than an audience is used to. Heather can't figure Shade out, as he constantly shifts and changes in her mind.

Using this visual breakdown approach, I was finally offered a feature film on 35mm. Admittedly, I was hired because I could provide the cheap camera rental. From my perspective, it had a wonderful budget (in truth it was only $300,000 but seemed huge to me at the time), some recognizable actors (actually a slightly known soap star who housewives fantasized about while folding husbands' socks), and was intended for theatrical release rather than straight to DVD.

This opportunity was my first introduction to the cruel world of cinematography, where filmmaking and business collide. I worked for a month of pre-production without a signed contract or financial compensation. Blinded by over-excitement, their verbal commitment was good enough for me. Twenty-four hours before principal photography was to begin, the producer pulled the plug and the film disappeared overnight. I took a huge financial hit, having spent a month in pre-production and turning down work for the following month designated for principal photography. That meant no income for two full months. As a result, I learned the importance of contracts.

Before taking that first job as a cinematographer, create a contract, usually referred to as deal memo. The purpose of this document is to:

1. Define the working terms agreed upon by yourself and the producer of the production. Make sure that it is clear, so there is no confusion down the line.

2. Protect yourself from being taken advantage of while under a producer's employment. There must be mutual understanding as to what is expected from both parties.

3. Solidify the professional approach and level of respect between yourself and the producer. It is more than a handshake or nod of agreement; rather, the deal memo is a piece of paper that can be used in a legal action when a party doesn't hold to their end of the bargain.

The following pages contain a standard deal memo I have used. Feel free to copy, cut, or paste any portion for your own use.

# – DEAL MEMO –

## 1. SERVICE FEE:

The PRODUCER agrees to pay Austin F. Schmidt $_____ per week for a total of _____ weeks for the production titled _____. This Deal Memo begins _____ and is completed on _____. The PRODUCER guarantees to pay Mr. Schmidt a "Kill Fee" in the amount of $_____ upon the signing of this Deal Memo, regardless of any event that prohibits the completion of the production.

## 2. SELF-PROMOTION:

Subject to performance, the PRODUCER shall accord main and/or end titles on a separate card (as it fits within the film's title structure). The card shall read:

Director of Photography – AUSTIN F. SCHMIDT

The PRODUCER must allow Mr. Schmidt:

- One (1) copy of digital master at the PRODUCER's expense.
- One (1) DVD copy of completed product once released and are commercially available at the PRODUCER's expense
- To select takes and still images from the highest quality HD or digital master at the PRODUCER's expense.
- Access to print and electronic press kits.

Mr. Schmidt agrees that materials will be used solely for his show reel, portfolio and promotion.

3. INSURANCE:
The PRODUCER shall provide liability insurance for any medical expenses acquired from work-related injuries.

4. WORKING HOURS:
Mr. Schmidt will work twelve (12) hours per day with a turn-around time of ten (10) hours. Any hours or part thereof in excess of twelve (12) hours per day shall increase payment to time and a half of the hourly breakdown. Any additional money is to be paid at the end of every week.

5. FOOD:
Mr. Schmidt is entitled to his meals at the PRODUCER's expense while working in any capacity for the production.

6. TRANSPORTATION:
Mr. Schmidt is entitled to compensation for any travel expenses accrued during the period of the Deal Memo, as well as any travel expenses pertaining to the PRODUCER's production before and after the Deal Memo is signed.

7. ARTISTIC CONTROL:
Mr. Schmidt will work in conjunction with the PRODUCER toward mutual approval on the selection of his crew, film stock, equipment, processing laboratory, and video transfer facility; provided that in the event of a conflict, the decision of the PRODUCER shall govern and control. Mr. Schmidt will be consulted on all 2nd Unit photography, plates, and all other photography on the production that may not be directly under his supervision. Mr. Schmidt has the right of first (1st) refusal regarding delayed or additional photography, to be paid at the same rate

agreed upon in this Deal Memo. The job of a cinematographer includes artistic control of the image through post-production. The PRODUCER will allow Mr. Schmidt this control during any answer-print of the film, along with any timing and/or color correction of the transfer to tape or any other process where color correction is to be implemented to the master tape for cable, television, video cassettes, DVDs, and laser discs.

## 8. ENTIRE AGREEMENT:
This Deal Memo expresses the entire arrangement between the parties; any changes must be made in writing.

## 9. ATTORNEY'S FEES:
In the event of litigation between the parties rising out of this Deal Memo, the prevailing party shall be entitled to recover reasonable attorney's fees and costs of suit.

I, _____, acknowledge that I have read and agree to adhere to the Deal Memo's stipulations outlined above. I acknowledge that any changes to the above-said contract will require a new contract to be written with all parties' approval and their signatures.

_____                    _____
(Producer's Signature)                              (Date)

An important aspect to the contract I provided above is stated in section 1. SERVICE FEE. In it you will find the mention of a "Kill Fee". A Kill Fee, or "Work Guarentee" means that no matter what happens to the production, you are to receive an agreed percentage of the full payment once the contract has been signed. This protects you from a producer's mistake that can result in a production being delayed or cancelled, like the feature I described earlier. After committing to a production, you must turn down others during that time. But when the production cancels, you have missed the ability to find other work for the pre-allotted time period and potential income is lost.

Once, I didn't receive a check for two weeks of work on a production that was cancelled as a result of an IRS audit. Because of that, I demanded the producer of the next feature agree to my Kill Fee, of which she made payment once the contract was signed. Production was cancelled after a week of shooting. Not a single crewmember was paid. Because of my original contract, however, I received some money due to the agreed upon Kill Fee. These stories show that no matter how good events may go in the beginning, change happens quickly and you never want to be left with the short end of the stick.

If a production does fall apart, the process of suing then collecting the owed money is another matter. The success rate of collecting your loss is pretty low. In truth, any contract you sign cannot force a producer to pay money that is owed. Hopefully it will scare them into doing so when confronted with small claims court or a collection agency.

In the world of independent filmmaking, a producer may never agree to the exact demands outlined above. A deal memo may change, depending on the particular needs and constraints of each production. Generally, they can't afford to pay a decent day rate, much less travel expenses or a copy of the film in the medium of your choice at their expense. Often you will sacrifice some of this security to work on the film, so always consider which is more important at the time, personal protection or the opportunity to work.

# — FEE NEGOTIATIONS —

When discussing work compensation, there are several forms to consider. The most common is physical payment during various periods of the film's production. Not all low-budget films can provide money, so they offer two other forms of compensation. One is called "Deferred Pay". Deferred Pay is a set amount of money agreed to by you and the production, which is paid to you if and when the film recoups its expenses, repays the financiers and begins to make money. There is a hierarchy to who receives the "Deferred Pay" first. The cinematographer is at the top of the list in front of other key crewmembers, but always behind the financiers, producer, and director. Negotiate as high a position as possible. You don't want the money to run out before it is your turn to receive Deferred Pay. The purpose of a production offering Deferred Pay is to entice a cinematographer to work, despite their inability to pay for the services up front. This is a risk and in my experience has never paid off. Everything depends on the success of the film. A film offering Deferred Pay alludes to its value level, as those involved hope for success in a film festival and possible distribution to pay back the financier's original investment. Even though the chance of receiving Deferred Pay is very low, negotiate for some. Who knows it could pay off some time. The other form of compensation is called "Points". In Hollywood, Points are spread between the financiers, directors, producers, and A-list actors. It is rare for a cinematographer to receive Points. However, Points are given to key crewmembers on independent films to entice commitment from more experienced individuals. The benefit of Points over Deferred Pay is that it represents a percentage of the film's profit, which will pay off while the film continues to make money over the negotiated period of time. You could collect payments from Points for several years. Daniel Pearl, ASC has said he still receives checks in the mail having accepted Points for shooting the original *Texas Chainsaw Massacre* some thirty-five years ago. The downside to Points over Deferred Pay is that they are only applicable once the Deferred Payments are made to those who negotiated for it.

First, negotiate for monetary compensation, then Deferred Pay and/or Points. It tells the producer you are serious about your work and that you expect everyone to treat your time and efforts with professionalism.

# THE REAL WORKING WORLD

In the land of Hollywood, it seems no one is anyone until they have agency representation or have joined a Union. A fog of mystery surrounds this element of the industry. Who are these people? What do they do exactly? How does one join? A certain crewmember claims this, while another declares that. Opinions give way to contradiction leaving the young cinematographer daunted by the vagueness of it all.

# – AGENTS –

At some point you will hear that the key to success begins with acquiring an agent. This myth has been running around the industry for quite some time. Let me be clear on this point: a cinematographer does not need an agent to become successful. Can it help? You bet. Is it a short-cut to higher profile jobs? It can be.

There never seems to be the perfect time at which to "get" an agent. I put this in quotations, because if your mindset is to "get" an agent, it means you aren't ready for one. If an agency has not approached you, that means your career is not proven enough from a financial standpoint to make it worth their while; hence the act of you approaching them is pointless and a waste of time. There have been a few examples when successful agent/client relationships have formed after a client takes the initiative, though rare. The first agency I signed with discovered me through one of their assistants. The agency was small and had existed for only a year or so. The assistant was a person I had known while attending NYU. She recommended me to the company's lead agent, and one month later, I signed with them. Simple as that. I didn't deserve it over other cinematographers, and I know for a fact there were others with marketable portfolios that weren't signed. But that's the way it goes in this business. The cliché rings true: who you know is just as important as what you know. When looking at an agency for representation, consider several things.

## How Big Is The Agency?

The last thing you want is to sign with an agency and get lost in a stockpile of clients. Huge companies such as International

Creative Management, United Talent Agency, and Paradigm are high-profile agencies. If you sign with a big agency, you may be assigned to a junior agent and are subject to their inexperience and lack of ability to negotiate work. These agencies spend time on their big fish who are likely to make them money. Their rational for signing a new cinematographer is the hope that the individual will have a breakout career and the agency will be a direct beneficiary of that success. If the cinematographer doesn't jumpstart from the gate, it will not hurt the agency. It is then merely an opportunity for their junior agent to build experience. I do not recommend signing with a big agency in the beginning; rather, a smaller one known as a boutique agency that will not forget your name. They have a vested interest in your future as the partnership rises together in success.

## Who Else Do They Represent?

Who an agency represents is indicative of their capability and their connections in the industry. If the agency roster is filled with cinematographers at your level, then it probably isn't a good idea to sign with them. It means this agency has no connections, no ability to find work, and little overall experience in the field of representation. The ideal agency represents a wide range in clients including feature, commercial, and music video, cinematographers, all with different experience levels, ranging from ASC members to new bloods such as yourself. They should also represent other production positions, most importantly line producers (LP). These individuals can have a direct hand in recommending and hiring crew. It becomes a symbiotic relationship as the agency negotiates a job for the LP, the LP will attempt to hire other crewmembers within the agency. An agency like this is beneficial to a young cinematographer providing exposure through association. If the need for a cinematographer arises, your reel will be cast in with the agency's few others, which becomes an opportunity to be seen that you didn't have before.

## Where Is The Agency Located?

This is a consideration that should never fully influence your decision, but is something of which to be aware. In this day and age, location seems to affect a person's success less and less. An agency in London can easily represent a client all the way in Japan. My first agency was based in New York, even though I had relocated to Los Angeles. At the time of signing, it didn't seem too far away and shouldn't have been a big deal. Rather quickly, however, I realized that all of their connections were New York-based, with few resources in the Los Angeles area. Oftentimes they put me up for jobs in which a New York production became interested and wanted an interview. "Mr. Schmidt is based in LA, so unfortunately he won't be able to make it to the interview. But he would be more than willing to participate in a conference call." By then, the production had seen a few cinematographers good enough for the job and the hassle of scheduling a conference call would not be worth it to them. And at this level, interviews are rarely about what is said; rather, the feeling and presence a production feels around the cinematographer are of utmost importance. How is that feeling and presence ever to be felt if everyone isn't in the same room together? Over the next six months, the agency became more recognized and they began cultivating relationships outside the New York area. Jobs started to come in from California and other states as well.

During the process of signing, I had a drink with an agency friend to get his opinion on the matter. What he said pertains to every young cinematographer's position.

It doesn't really matter if I've heard of them (referring to the agency I signed with). Right now, at this point in your career it is better to sign with an agency for a year and see what happens. After that, you can leave. What's one year in a lifetime career? Nothing. Worst-case scenario, you walk away having learned more about the business side of things and maybe how to do it better next time. It's always harder to get your first agent than your second. If you decide to move on to another, you will look more enticing because at one point somebody else wanted you, so you must not be all that bad.

If you have a choice between agencies, then do consider their size, who they represent, and their location. If only one is knocking on the door, then remember, it is much harder to get your first agent than your second.

The main job of an agency is to negotiate contractual and financial issues and act as a buffer between you and the potential production regarding contract terms, payments, and performance requirements. If a cinematographer handles these delicate issues, his or her relationship with the production can become touchy and a bit strained. An agent takes all the nastiness into his or her hands, allowing you to focus with the production on work itself. An added bonus is that the agent often negotiates for harder terms from a more distanced perspective, which can benefit you with higher monetary compensation.

Signing with an agency also has the advantage of appearing accomplished and professional to any prospective director or producer. An agency does not sign someone without a competent and successful track record. This ensures a producer or director of your experience level compared to other cinematographers who don't have representation. A production will sometimes go directly to an agent in order to feel confident with their selection process, instead of culling through massive piles of suspicious submissions.

I had always assumed that having an agent would benefit me from the "trickle down" effect. If an agency has booked their top cinematographers, then I would get bumped up to higher-profile productions since I would be the only person available. I have heard of this happening, but not as often as I once believed. If a production is not able to sign a certain cinematographer, they move on to the next agency and are not necessarily willing to take the risk on a lesser-known cinematographer. The only time the "trickle down" effect has worked for me was when the agency had packaged together several of their below-the-line talents into a monetary deal for the production.

Naturally, nothing in this world is for free, certainly not in the film business. Agents receive a percentage of your earnings, ranging from 10% to 20%. This percentage includes work that you have acquired yourself, whether the agency negotiated it or not. This is a significant consideration in the beginning of your career and may affect the timing of when to sign. Until you gain some notoriety, jobs rarely come through the agency. At this time, you may not be able to afford giving up ten percent of the income from jobs that you secured without the agency's help.

There are always additional fees charged when marketing you through DVD reels, mailing submissions, and hosting online material for clients to instantly access. An agency's main concern is to promote you using the best quality possible. This places your work in hands that you wouldn't otherwise have access to. But consider whether it is costing more than it is worth. Ensure they are not making money while promoting and that the extra costs are actually going to what they are spending your fees on. When signing with an agent, don't be too hasty. Be certain it benefits you. You are employing them for their services, not the other way around. Otherwise, what's the point in surrendering that ten percent?

# — THE UNION —

The story of the International Cinematographers Guild (ICG), also known as Local 600, began sometime ago when several cameramen met in kitchens to organize the first photographers' local. While films created headline stars out of directors and actors, cinematographers and their crews dissolved into the background. Technological advances of the 1920's allowed industry migration from its original confines in and around New York and Chicago to the wide-open space of Los Angeles. This development resulted in more work for more camera people in more parts of the country. At the time, cinematographers barely earned $25 a week. Cameramen turned to the International Alliance of Theatrical Stage Employees (IATSE) for help.

East Coast Local 644 was chartered in New York City in 1926, followed by Local 659 in Los Angeles in 1928 and Local 666 in Chicago in 1929 and camera crews finally had a voice at the negotiating table.

By the 1930's, Hollywood studios had cinematographers under contract along with the actors, writers, directors and other key players. Individuals were hired by the job but advanced very slowly, usually when someone retired or died. The Union took on small fights, but often lost to the more powerful Hollywood heads.

The introduction of television changed the game and created additional opportunities for cinematographers. Despite this resulting increase in work, practices like closed industry rosters and standbys were obvious signs of tension between the three geographically-divided camera locals. For years, the locals routinely ignored their own procedures for allowing members to transfer from one local to another, claiming they could not accommodate any new members. As frustration amongst the members grew, so did their sentiment for a merger.

To compete with television, studios spent the better part of the '60's and '70's developing the formula for "blockbuster films", and by utilizing lighter camera equipment, began shooting movies in multiple locations around the country. As a result, the old studio system and their contracts for stars, writers, directors and cinematographers came to a close. Jurisdictional disputes between the three camera locals continued through the '80's.

In 1989, Local 659 opened the Guild to all qualified people, laying the groundwork for establishing the national local. On May 16, 1996, the three locals merged together and created IATSE Local 600, the International Cinematographers Guild (ICG). By 1998, 93% of the voting membership ratified the first-ever national camera contract. Local 600 is now a national Guild with three regions. The National office in Los Angeles handles California and the 13 Western states. The Central Region Offices are located in Chicago and Miami with coverage from Illinois to the Gulf Stream. The Eastern Region Office covers New York and the remaining Eastern states.

Local 600 is an affiliate of IATSE, the international union that represents the skilled crafts in the world of filmmaking. IATSE protects the common interest of its members throughout the United States, Canada and Puerto Rico. It negotiates most working contracts, protects members with safety and health regulations, prevents producer exploitation and provides health and retirement plans. This unity increases the bargaining strength of the local unions.

All prospective Union persons should become familiar with the Contract Services Administration Trust Fund (CSATF). They oversee the Industry Experience and Television/Commercial Rosters and the Safety Pass Training Program, which currently applies to the Western region only.

The Industry Experience Roster (IER) is a list of individuals who have proven work experience in a specific job classification in the motion picture industry. Placement on this roster allows an individual to work on any motion picture project-feature, episodic television, music video, or commercial. There are two ways to become eligible for placement on the IER. You may accumulate 30 Union days working in one job classification within a year. The second way is to work 100 non-Union days over a three-year period in one camera classification. Any work that is considered must be paid and performed in the United States. Proof of these days must be supported by payroll and production records and/or employer letters verifying employment.

The Television Commercial Roster (TCR) is distinctly different in that individuals on that roster can only work on Union commercials. A prospective member can apply once they have worked 30 days in his/her job classification. Accruing 90 additional days in the same job classification enables one to join the IER and work on any feature, music video, commercial, episodic television. Proof of work days for the TCR are exactly like the IER; through payroll and production records and/or employer letters verifying employment.

Once roster status has been approved, the CSATF will notify the National Office and in turn, Local 600 will invite that individual to join. A prospective member should immediately contact the National Office telling of his/her desire to join and will be allowed to do so with a down payment on the initiation fee and by attending new member orientation meetings. As Local 600 and CSATF are separate entities, it is up to the individual to contact both the CSATF and Local 600.

To join Local 600 through the Eastern Office, similar proof of experience and work days are required, but unlike the Western and Central regions, the process begins and ends in the Eastern region office. To join in the Central region, one must provide a resume and credit list to prove work experience in their desired classification. There are no other set requirements. The Central Office evaluates a prospective member's ability on a case-by-case basis. However, Local 600 representatives always recommend a prospective member to apply to CSATF, in case the individual has the opportunity to work in the Western states. It would be a shame to give up a job because you were negligent in taking that extra step.

There is no ideal time to submit to CSATF and Local 600. Only until you have worked a sufficient number of days does it make sense to apply. Consider your financial status and number of opportunities to work Union jobs. The money made from one Union production doesn't always justify paying the initiation fee and annual dues. Consistent Union work gradually happens over time. The budgets of movies you are hired for will continue to increase as producers and directors you work with elevate to work within Union jobs.

Membership in Local 600 requires an initiation fee, quarterly dues and a 1% assessment on gross wages. Payments vary depending on the job classification. For instance, the fee and dues for an assistant cameraperson is less than for a Director of Photography. Also, a person may only hold one job classification at a time. If a person classified as a camera assistant wishes to re-rate to camera operator, they need only pay the difference in membership fee and increase in dues.

When a production is non-Union, producers do not expect to be held to Union guidelines. They may ignore overtime, meal penalties, and general safety guidelines. However, crewmembers come to expect many of these conditions to be met, whether the production is Union or not. Rules should be clarified contractually before stepping onto any set.

Ultimately it is your responsibility to keep a production accountable. If expensive film equipment is being used, star actors are part of the cast, or other high-price elements are in place, yet your day rate is barely more than that of a pizza delivery person, the show could potentially qualify to become a Union production and flip. If you feel that you are being taken advantage of, call Local 600. Every caller, whether a member or not, can be assured their personal information is kept confidential so as not to jeopardize his/her future working relationships.

Once you have reported the production to Local 600, they will in turn report to IATSE. IATSE will then determine whether the production should become Union and will notify all the other Locals of their decision.

IATSE has become more cognizant of the amount of work going to their members on small shows. As a result of shrinking production budgets, the Union has had to lower its demands on production in regard to contracts. Union members are allowed to work on non-Union shows; however, they are required to report the job to the Union. This allows the Union to be aware of the work being performed.

The purpose of IATSE is to protect their people, not shut down low-budget productions. They want everyone to work. The overall budget is not the determining factor, the production's ability to operate while under Union guidelines is. If ordering a production to turn Union means the production will have to shut down, thus preventing individuals from working, then they might not get involved.

The Union is strictly there for YOU. If questions arise in your career and certain situations need to be addressed, call them directly. Their representatives are generous people willing to take time to ensure that you are comfortable in the profession you have chosen.

# FIRST FEATURE PRODUCTION JOURNAL

The summer before signing with my first agency, I began pre-production on *Backstreets of Heaven*, my first endeavor into the world of feature filmmaking.

To this day, I have no idea how the Director discovered me. I had never heard of his film, nor had I submitted my work to any ads he placed online. I received his first phone call in March, and we occasionally touched base during the following months through email and over the phone. His captivating script fueled my enthusiasm. The technical and visual challenges would allow me to showcase what I had trained for over the years. Though it was the Director's first film and he would be playing the lead role, his passion and dedication erased any cautionary red flags.

Barstow, California.

Summer in the Mojave.

Trapped in a town run by crime lords, Zee and Red must complete one final drug delivery to earn their freedom. With money and love at stake, this is the two friend's last chance at redemption. But nothing ever goes as planned in the hot desert sun.

In truth, it was a well-written action story: beautiful landscapes, pyrotechnics, car crashes, and blazing gunfights. Not your typical first-feature fare. I created my usual visual breakdown before our first meeting.

# – VISUAL BREAKDOWN –

– Color: The desert backdrop is vast, barren, and lifeless at first glance. Create depth using contrasting colors. Cool colors naturally recede while warm colors pop out. Use this to our advantage. Make the desert cool while warming the actors in the foreground. This creates visual depth and motivates the characters. Though our heroes are familiar with the town of Barstow, it has never felt like home. An emotional chasm separates them from their desert surroundings. This separation permeates the interiors as well. The desert light invades through cool windows; however, the interior lights and practicals remain warm. One exception is the crime boss' office, where a steel green hue from overhead will create a dirty industrial look, alluding to evil and lawless deeds, which birthed our heroes' problems. Costuming should continue this color scheme. No bright colors can be worn; all dull as if eaten by the sun's intense rays. Nothing can conflict with the constant presence of blood. Red should never appear, so that when red blood flows this color stands out from its lack of presence anywhere else.

– Atmosphere: This creates distinct separation between interiors and the exteriors. The surroundings are never comfortable, but places of unfamiliarity. Interior haze introduces a suffocating and restrictive feeling. For the exteriors, no overheads will be used to soften the sun. Allow the harsh rays to beat down, creating hard shadows and edges.

– Lenses: Each focal length has unique characteristics. Wide lens characteristics, such as little image compression and wide depth-of-field, establish friendship and camaraderie between our three heroes. Long lens characteristics of increased image compression and shallow depth-of-field portray selfishness and individualism in the "bad" guys. This allows the opportunity to alternate imagery, depending on a character's internal fight between good and evil. The audience will never notice, but they will feel it. Almost like subliminal advertising. You don't know what you just read, but by god a Coke sure would taste good right now.

– Camera Movement: Each action sequence and stunt is covered with smooth hand-held for reasons of speed and "realism". Every other scene will be punctuated with vertical and horizontal jib work. Static shots are used only when there is room limitation or on-set time constraints.

After the Director read the breakdown, we met at a coffee shop in Hollywood and a contract was immediately struck: $150 per day for 18 shooting days; $1,800 in deferred pay and 3 producer's points. Pre-production began.

# – PRE-PRODUCTION –

## Testing

Camera tests before every feature film are vital in creating a visual look. They show every person in production the director and cinematographer's intentions. Test film stocks, cameras, and post workflow to see which provides the "look" you desire and best suits the production's need. Experiment with filtration techniques if necessary. Perform latitude tests to learn how much you can under or over light the image. Observe how wardrobe and makeup appear under the lighting conditions you will use. Case in point, I own a pair of pants that appear washed-out gray in sunlight. Once inside, the pants reflect hunter green. If shot on film, it may appear the actor made a wardrobe change every time he or she walked in and out of a house. Some materials reflect light differently, depending on the light source. Be aware of this before approving wardrobe choices. This is also true for makeup. What may look good to your eye may appear different on the chosen film stock. Tests guard against surprises in dailies.

Because the budget for this film was so low, we could not afford camera tests. We walked onto set with only my experience as a basis for judgment. This is quite typical for low-budget films. If you are uncomfortable with this, it is up to you to learn what's necessary to prevent ill-wanted surprises when screening footage later. That means you may have to test on your own dime. Bad footage is a poor reflection on you as a cinematographer.

## Film Stock

The film negative chosen was Kodak's Vision 2 100T 7212 and Vision 2 500T 7218. Both are tungsten-balanced stocks. The 7218 was intended for the few interior locations, as they provided little natural light and our lighting package was small. When shooting S16mm, I prefer to use the slowest film speed possible such as the 7212. Not much difference is seen between slow and fast speed stocks on a television monitor, but once projected onto a big screen, image quality is easily discernable. Slower stocks keep the image sharper and less grainy. If additional grain is needed, the blow-up to 35mm print will certainly provide that. Grain is a beautiful characteristic of film, but there is a point when it stops being an aesthetic choice and becomes a distraction. I could have used an even slower film stock, Vision 2 50D 7201, but it is daylight-balanced. This would require an additional filter package. The budget didn't allow for multiple filter packages, plus it costs additional set time when switching between them.

Our first stock purchase was in the amount of 17,600 feet. This was based on a 4:1 shooting ratio, all the budget could afford. For our 110-minute movie, we would have only 440 minutes of film to capture the entire story. This was an extremely low footage count, as most low-budget films shoot with at least a 7:1 shooting ratio. This low shooting ratio also concerned me, because of the amount of action sequences the script required. With two cameras running during those times, we were bound to shoot more than a normal narrative feature.

## Camera Package

The "A" camera equipment package is included below. It is presented in a useful, organized list to submit to a rental house. Provide every detail and be neat. This prevents miscommunication in pre-production.

Camera
- Arri SR2 Super 16mm PL lens mount w/ 1:1.85 ground glass

Zoom Lens
- 8-64mm Canon T2.4 in PL mount

Camera Accessories
- 3   400' magazines
- 3   onboard batteries and charger
- 2   battery blocks
- 1   4x5.6 swing-away matte box 2x tray, 1 rotating
- 1   follow focus unit
- 1   whip
- 1   crank
- 1   right-hand grip handle

Video Assist Accessories
- 1   onboard monitor
- 1   8" field monitor w/ 25', 50' BNC chords

Support
- 1   Ronford F15S fluid head Mitchell based
- 1   standard legs
- 1   baby legs
- 1   high hat

We deliberated early on whether to use the Director's personal camera package, an Éclair NPR. I knew the Éclair could work; however, as discussions progressed, I changed my mind. The Éclair presented several problems that would consume precious time on set, mainly as a result of the camera's lack of video tap. The Director could not watch a shot on monitor. Ultimately we decided to rent an Arri SR2 package, making it our "A" camera and using the Éclair as a "B" camera for the stunt and action sequences. The Stunt Coordinator also had an Éclair package which served as our "C" camera, to be used for one-time-only stunts. I chose not to use prime lenses, and opted for a quality zoom lens instead. Speed was top on my mind. Lens changes take time. Shooting with a zoom lens allows quick changes to the frame when capturing action sequences. The desert was also a factor. Anytime a lens is removed or a magazine changed, it allows dust and foreign particles to enter the camera gate, creating scratches on the film negative.

### Filter Package

4x5.6 filters:

- ·1   85
- ·1   81B
- ·1   ND series (.3, .6, .9, 1.2)
- ·2   optical flats
- ·1   linear polarizer

I faced several challenges pertaining to filter usage. I needed to create cool backgrounds and warm foregrounds with little to no lighting equipment. This had to be done with color correction filters. Also, during action sequences, flying debris might hit the lens. Though optical flats (clear pieces of glass) are used for protection, we couldn't risk breaking a color correction filter since there was only one set. I needed to create the look of the movie without endangering the filters. In the desert, light reflects off the clouds, sand and rocks; basically everything in sight. Too many filters might cause light to refract off their surfaces into the lens. This creates imperfections on the negative, such as double imaging. I needed to shoot with the least amount of filters in front of the lens to prevent that.

Ultimately, these challenges were solved with the same solution, a gray card. When processed film is sent to a post-facility for color correction, the colorist uses a gray card as a standard color and exposure reference. This is one way for a cinematographer to communicate to the colorist how the shot should look. If the gray card does not appear correct, the colorist introduces colors to the card until it appears the standard gray. These introduced colors then affect the photographed images proceeding after the gray card.

Before each tungsten film roll, I exposed the gray card to daylight with the 81B warming filter in front of the lens. The 81B filter is less warm than the 85 (the standard color-correcting filter when shooting tungsten film in daylight). The 81B does not fully correct the daylight color temperature exposing the tungsten-balanced film, leaving the image slightly cool. After shooting the gray card, I then pulled the 81B and shot the film sequences with this one less color correction filter. When viewing the gray card, the colorist would see it partially blue and add warmth to balance it. Because I pulled the 81B when shooting the sequences, the added warmth from the gray card would carry over the following images and result in a slightly cooler image. By utilizing this technique, I achieved the movie's cool look to the backgrounds, didn't risk the color correction filters, and used fewer filters in front of the lens.

## F/Stops

I prefer to keep my f/stops consistent throughout a shoot. Sometimes they differ from interior to exterior, but I decide what they are before filming begins. I plan the filter package and electric needs around this decision. If a slower f/stop is desired, then more powerful lighting units are ordered or less Neutral Density (ND) filtration is used. And vice versa for a faster f/stop. In truth, I habitually shoot most films at the same f/stop. There comes a time in a cinematographer's career when his or her dependence on a light meter becomes less and less. When I first began shooting, I metered every light on set. My eye was not trained to judge contrast levels. Over time confidence grows and your meter remains in its holster, only used to establish the key light, and everything else is judged by eye. To accomplish this, a lens must remain at a consistent f/stop. Otherwise, exposure will range from shot to shot and the light meter must be utilized more often than your trained eye. For most films, I shoot exteriors between an f/4 and f/5.6 depending on the sun's direction and brightness. In interiors, I shoot at an f/2.8. My eyes have become accustomed to these light levels. Instead of metering every light, my eye does the work, saving time on set. This consistency in f/stop would prove useful when shooting the exterior action sequences. I might find myself operating while light levels changed overhead. Rather than halting the set to take a light meter reading, I could look through the viewfinder to judge the light level and adjust the f/stop accordingly.

## Grip & Electric Package

The aesthetic look of the film didn't require an extensive electric and grip package. The desert would be extremely hot, leaving the crew to drag and walk listlessly as they worked. The package needed to be small and not cause any unnecessary hauling of equipment. Below is the electric and grip package.

ELECTRIC PACKAGE

Power and Distribution

- 2   Edison quad boxes
- 10 25' Edison stingers 12/3
- 5   50' Edison stingers 12/3

HMI Par

- 2   1.2k HMI Par (magnetic ballast, 2 header cables & spare globe)

KINO

- 2   2'x4 bank KINO FLO (tungsten and daylight globes)

Tungsten

- 2   26 degree Source 4 Lekos
- 2   LTM 420 peppers

GRIP PACKAGE

Stands

- 6   beefy baby 3-riser
- 2   primi baby stands
- 6   combo stands
- 10 c-stands
- 2   baby c-stands
- 1   high roller

Reflectors

- 2   4'x4' silver reflectors (hard/soft speckled)

Frames & Rags

- 1   8'x8' frame (w/ears)
- 2   6'x6' frame (w/ears)
- 1   8'x8' checkerboard (gold/silver)
- 2   6'x6' sold
- 1   6'x6' ultra bounce

Flags & Nets

- 4   4'x4' floppy flags
- 2   4'x4' empty flag frames
- 4   24"x36" solid flags
- 2   24"x36" grip doubles
- 2   24"x36" grip singles
- 2   24"x36" full silks
- 4   18"x24" solid flags
- 2   18"x24" grip double
- 2   18"x24" grip single

Hardware

- 6   lollipops
- 6   cardellinis
- 2   duckbills/platypus
- 2   baby pipe clamp (male)
- 6   ratchet straps
- 4   baby plates
- 1   butt plug
- 4   safety chains
- 2   sets wall spreaders for speed rail

- 1  8' speed rail
- 1  6' speed rail
- 10  grip clips (#1)
- 10  grip clips (#2)
- 6  grip clips (#3)

Wood
- 1  crate wedges
- 1  spindle bassa blocks (small)
- 4  full apple boxes
- 4  half apple boxes
- 4  quarter apple boxes
- 4  pancake apple boxes

Miscellaneous
- 15  35lb sandbags
- 10  20lb shot bags
- 4  furniture pads
- 1  sledgehammer
- 2  shovels
- 1  rake
- 1  push broom
- 6  bull pricks

Camera Mounts
- 1  long valley 7 jib mitchell based
         *150mm to 100m adapter
- 1  PD1 dolly

Carts
- 1  c-stand cart
- 1  muscle cart

Typically when filming outdoors, one utilizes big diffusion materials overhead to soften the sun as it directly hits the actors. I did not want to use this approach; rather, let the sun beat down on them unimpeded. Aesthetically the harsh lines and deep shadows created by the sun would fit more into the "look" that was intended. Also, "flying" overheads require substantial time and a large amount of crew, neither of which we had.

Creating cool backgrounds was solved through filtration, but adding warmth to the foreground had to be accomplished through our lighting package. There were several ways to add warmth, such as HMI lights or reflector boards directed through CTO frames. These were impractical for us given the budget and crew. Perhaps bounced sunlight off sheets of unbleached muslin might work. Unfortunately, muslin would not have the punch needed when set at a far distance from the subject. Maybe checkerboard material, which is square pieces of silver and gold lamé material sewn together, would do. But checkerboard creates too harsh of a light. The solution presented itself two weeks before principal photography began, when I flew up to Oregon for my sister's wedding. My brother, Brad, had offered for us both to photograph the wedding. I was not keen on this for several reasons, but sucked it up, as it seemed to make her happy. We hoped to make the shots pretty despite the circumstances, as the sky overhead was cloudy and created a flat look to the wedding pictures. Spying a cream-colored tablecloth at a catering station, I swiped it from the table and stretched it across an expandable piece of fencing to create a malleable reflector. Instant success! As Brad cajoled individuals into place, I squeezed the cloth close to the lens, reflecting a soft warm light beautifully onto their faces. Only after returning to Los Angeles did I realize I had stumbled onto the solution to my problem. My mother contacted the catering company, asking if they might sell the tablecloths. They laughed aloud and couldn't help but say "yes", as it was the most unusual request they had ever received. Fortunately the material arrived the day before leaving for Barstow. So, what was it about these cloths that made them so special? It came down to the cotton and polyester material. The cotton reflected a soft warming color like unbleached muslin, and had the throw of checkerboard as a result of the polyester sheen.

## Crew

Production constantly assured me that there were plenty of local crewmembers to fill positions in the various departments. I asked to bring some of my usual crewmembers from Los Angeles, but Production could only afford a low sum, if anything for them. One gaffer came out as a favor and a 2$^{nd}$ AC came out for the experience. A New York camera operator flew himself over as well. Otherwise, the task of filling crew positions was left to the Line Producer. I was hesitant of his ability to do so, doubting Barstow would have qualified personnel. But in my excitement to be a part of the production, I didn't press my concerns any further.

## Stunts

The Stunt Coordinator and his team were pulling out all the stops for this show. Their experience dated back to older days of television with the *Dukes of Hazzard*. I wanted to capture their efforts in the most exhilarating way possible. We obviously didn't possess the six-camera setup ability of Michael Bay, but did plan to shoot with two. There wasn't enough time in pre-production to fully grasp the challenges of each stunt or where the best place to shoot from might be. The Director, Stunt Coordinator and I did spend one day walking through an elaborate shootout scene. This made me aware of the possibilities of what we could do, and the time it would take to do it in. A lot of the camera work for the stunt sequences would be discovered right before a walk-through of the shooting day. Each stunt would be done twice, only three times if necessary. This is not the way to approach a heavy stunt film, whether it is your first or your twentieth. There are too many variables in how things may go down. The Director and I had very little time to plan, which left the door wide open for missed opportunities and mistakes.

We spent a day becoming accustomed to the weaponry used in the scenes. Safety was the biggest concern for the stunt team, having experienced a multitude of accidents over their careers. Because of these accidents, the Stunt Coordinator had designed new safety features used prevalently in Hollywood today. This included the "side blow" pistol where gasses blow out the side with the spent cartridge instead of the front of the barrel. This design was inspired by his connection to Brandon Lee's death, as a result of a firearm that emitted out the front. The side blow design provides safety for actors next to one another in the heat of battle, and allows the camera to film safely in front of the action. Standing in an interior location, the Stunt Coordinator fired a few rounds in close proximity to get me comfortable. I think I shit myself. Having grown up around guns in Colorado, I was used to them in outdoor hunting situations. But in this tiny enclosed space, the sound of the shots pounded off the walls and ringed inside my head. He chuckled at my reaction then pointed to my ears. I had forgotten to put my earplugs in.

## Paperwork

Detailed facts must be recorded, on which to base your next decisions and to learn from the decisions that were made. These detailed facts are vital to success. With camera notes and lighting diagrams, a cinematographer can duplicate a "look" when filming different locations. Most features require re-shoots or pick-ups long after principal photography is complete. This footage must match what was already shot. You may not be present for those days and another cinematographer steps in. It is impossible for them to continue your quality of work without detailed records to follow.

For each shot, the camera department should take note of:
1. Filters used;
2. F/stop;
3. Lens' focal length;
4. Lens' height; and
5. Camera angle in relation to subject.

For each scene, the electric department should take note of:
1. Which lighting units were used;
2. Where the units were placed;
3. What angles they were focused at;
4. Types of diffusion or gels applied;
5. Lighting contrast ratio; and
6. Light readings where applicable.

A valuable tool available to the cinematographer is a quality digital SLR still camera. The camera can record the approximate look of a shot to help duplicate it later. Paperwork can only get you so far and leaves room for interpretation. If the digital still camera is set up properly to mimic the setting of the stock's ASA, shutter speed, and f/stop, then its image will speak a thousand words.

## The Lab and Transfer Facility

Communication between the lab, transfer facility, and yourself is extremely important. In the film to digital process, steps are easily misinterpreted, resulting in less-than-quality images. An exact language of communication must be defined by all parties early and often in the pre-production stage. For this film, there was little communication, as Production had not decided on a post-house until after we began shooting. As a result, I made decisions that gave us flexibility in post, regardless of which route the Director might take in the end. Unfortunately, this approach does allow other people with little understanding of the "looks" created to manipulate the image without your input. They make un-educated decisions, diminishing the value of your personal touch on the final film.

## – PRINCIPAL PHOTOGRAPHY –

No matter the amount of planning spent during pre-production, events never occur the exact way in which you imagined. That is one reason why I love this job. No film is ever the same. Principal photography forces you to think on your toes, and this production required just that. Earlier I described how things were planned. The following is what actually happened.

### Film Stock

As predicted, we ran into stock quantity issues and shot well over the 4:1 ratio. Ultimately we used 40,000 feet, which is still an unbelievably low amount to cut an action feature. Even if we had budgeted for more though, there wasn't enough time in our schedule to shoot more.

### Camera Package

As the days progressed, we began shooting most scenes with multiple cameras to save time and allow for more coverage. Using a zoom lens was one of my better decisions, since we were under-manned and constantly roving during the shots. With only one AC left, as the 1st and myself were both operating cameras, there was never time to change lenses on either camera for each shot. While shooting, the "B" camera operator pulled his own focus. Not changing lenses also proved beneficial, as there were very little to no scratches reported by the lab. Desert heat fried out the video tap on "A" camera in week one. Because Barstow was too far from a rental house to get a replacement, we worked without it. Instead, the Director had trusted me with framing.

## Filter Package

I was never allowed to see the footage transferred off the negative at the post facility. The reason for this is described later. As a result, I don't know if my filter practices aided the "look" of the final image and cannot comment on the success of the techniques utilized.

## F/Stops

Unfortunately, I wasn't always consistent with the f/stop in each scene. One day, while perched on top of a hill and framing an establishing shot of the picture car driving down the freeway, the ND3 filter popped out of its spring lock. The glass seemed to fall in slow motion, as the 1st AC and I juggled it between our hands, until it shattered on the rocky ground. Without a backup, I was forced to compensate by altering the lens stop. This didn't hurt the image quality, but made several moments uncomfortable for me when making split-second decisions. Cinematographers are superstitious and love the comfort of familiarity. I am no exception. Interiors were shot at an f/2.8; however, exteriors ranged from an f/4 to an f/8. This resulted in inconsistent exposures between shots, since my eye could not judge continuity through the viewfinder when there was not time to pull out a light meter.

## Grip & Electric Package

Desert conditions changed constantly. In an instant, winds swirled around us, picking up tents and anything not fully secured down. This wind would have presented a huge problem had we been "flying" overheads above the actors. The tablecloth proved to be the workhorse, providing the exact look I wanted while being lightweight and easy for the crew to move around. When lighting exteriors, we kept it very simple. Any type of kickers or highlights were created with reflecting silver boards. Negative fill was done with 4'x4' floppies. And our key or fill light was bounced from the cream-colored tablecloth. Lighting the interiors to match outside was just as simple. HMI lights blasting through windows created our cool background, while Kinoflos mixed with daylight and tungsten bulbs matched the warmth of the tablecloth.

## Crew

The Line Producer was successful in securing several crewmembers from the Barstow local. However, none of them had film set experience. Not only were they filling multiple crew positions, they were also utilized as actors. This complicated matters by disrupting the orderly flow of a working set in which I had always been accustomed to. Naturally, it was challenging to shoot an action film using three cameras with only fifteen people. That being said, I was amazed with the crew's work effort day in and day out. By the end of the shoot, they had become hardened and experienced production people. The lead actors even pitched in, picking up sandbags and packing equipment with the rest of us.

## Stunts

As the 1st AC described it, "There's nothing quite like operating a camera inside a car while the stunt man from *Dukes of Hazzard* is at the wheel." Many times, I found myself only feet from blasting guns and exploding body squibs. One such time, Red and Zee were instructed to run from a building under gunfire. Small detonation charges were placed in the door while the stunt crew stood off camera with paint ball guns, their ammunition filled with dirt to look like bullet hits. Action was called, the charges blew, and the actors ran out the door with guns blazing. I quickly ran in to capture the action up close, but noticed through my viewfinder that they had veered from the original planned path and were coming directly at me. Jacked up on anxiety, adrenaline and testosterone, combined with loud explosions, no wonder they forgot which way to go. Not seeing me three feet to their right, they continued firing away at the "bad guys". Even though the bullets are blank, crew is wearing protection, and everyone believes they're going to live to see the next day, these types of shots feel pretty damn realistic. Not wanting to turn and blindly run the other direction, as that might cause more problems, I stood still, closed my eyes and wrapped my left hand over my head. A sudden wash of heat from the explosions hit. The acidic taste of gunpowder layered itself on my tongue. Paintballs whizzed through the air. Holy shit! Is this for real? I'm going to get shot! Bang, Bang, Bang. No earplugs could block the gun's noise at such a close range. I shrunk as small as possible, and continued to point the camera in the direction of the blasts passing by. With all the intensity of the moment, no one realized I was there. Unscathed, I quietly walked away, a little shook up.

The Stunt Coordinator constantly said, "If one of my guys isn't bleeding, then the day isn't over yet." We assumed the majority of accidents might occur while filming the climactic action scenes that were scheduled to shoot during the final week. A stunt motorcyclist was to drive with shotgun in hand, fire at our escaping heroes, crash into a pile of barrels, fly over the handle bars, and immediately stand up to resume shooting. Zee then was to fire a shot at the gas-filled barrels, igniting them and the stuntman into a ball of fire. The Stunt Coordinator ordered everyone to stand in silence. The stunt crew dripped flammable cement glue over the burn-man's body. The Stunt Coordinator turned toward the burn-man, said a quick prayer, then hugged and kissed his forehead. "I'll see you when you're done." The hood was closed and sealed with duck tape. A person set on fire must have his clothing and other attire completely sealed to prevent flames from traveling inside the suit. This also means the burn-man is holding his breath as soon as the helmet is taped shut. We began rolling the three cameras, and whoosh, the cement glue ignited. The burn-man stood up from the wreck, advancing toward us, shotgun blazing. Three, four, five rounds were ejected before the Stunt Coordinator shouted, "DOWN! And cut!" The stunt crew ran in to extinguish the flames while ripping open the fire suit. The burn-man came out panting and gasping for air to the applause of everyone around. Pretty damn intense, I can tell you that much. He received 2nd degree burns on his hands. Apparently a man on fire needs the use of his hands to flail, keeping the suit cool; however, the shotgun deterred him from doing so. He was aware this might happen, but did it any way. Those guys were definitely adrenaline junkies.

Other than that, the entire week of stunts continued with only a few scrapes and bruises. Despite this successful run, our minds weren't eased as the final day approached. The climactic car chase scene required a head-on collision between the heroes and local crime boss. The chase sequence had already been shot. All that remained was the final moment of impact. It was decided that only one car would move, therefore limiting the variables and potential danger with two drivers involved. The rest would be solved in the editing room. One picture car was parked above a ten-foot riverbed wall. The Stunt Coordinator planned to barrel into its right side just in front of the front passenger wheel at 50mph. Both cars would then fly off the riverbed wall in a ball of dust. I perched "A" camera on top of a production truck to capture an overhead view of the crash. We weren't sure if either car would flip over on the roof or roll on the ground, so with that in mind, "B" camera was placed outside the landing zone but close enough to alter the shot depending on the crash result. "C" camera was rigged inside the Stunt Coordinator's car with a view out the front windshield for personal perspective of the stunt.

It was to be the Stunt Coordinator's last stunt performance of his career. He had a special dinner with his family the night before, and his wife now watched the event with a choice cocktail concoction in her hand. She was used to this, but it still made her nervous. The Stunt Coordinator hadn't had a great history when it came to performing car stunts. At the beginning of his career, he drove the General Lee for the *Dukes of Hazzard* TV series. One particular jump sent the car's nose falling forward to the ground, the engine pushing itself and the Stunt Coordinator all the way to the back seat an instant after impact. It took years of multiple surgeries and ongoing rehab to get him out of the hospital. Having viewed a press clipping of the accident, it looked as if the car had been compressed from nose to trunk by a machine. Still, accidents such as that hadn't deterred him over the years, and he was excited for this to be his last stunt. Each member of the stunt crew knew their role if the stunt went wrong. One role is that of the entry-man. His job is to use a crow bar to pry open a car in case access to the inside is blocked or crushed. The skill of the entry-man can make the difference between life or death for the driver. For this occasion, the Stunt Coordinator asked that his 18 year-old son be given the responsibility. Several stunt crewmembers asked him to reconsider. The Stunt Coordinator only replied, "He's gotta learn sometime." He kissed his wife and said a quick prayer with the stunt team while everyone stood in silence. EMTs stood nearby. The

Stunt Coordinator climbed through the car window and reversed slowly to the starting position. Cameras began rolling. "And Action!" The car's engine roared to life, getting closer and closer to final impact. It crashed with a loud noise, throwing up a huge dust storm. Then stillness. "And Cut!" Stunt crew rushed in. The Stunt Coordinator made no response to their calls. "Get the entry-man." The Stunt Coordinator's son began prying open the back hatch. EMTs supported the Stunt Coordinator's head with their hands. Still no reaction. The son couldn't open the back trunk. He was too small, without enough body weight to pressure the latch open. It was painful watching the son unable to save his dad. Too much time was wasting. "Get him off!" Another stunt man pushed him aside. The desert was dead silent. Only grunting sounds from the new entry-man and the calming voices of the EMTs attempting to coax the Stunt Coordinator alive were heard. Initially, "B" camera was instructed to continue rolling after cut had been yelled. The Director wanted us to film the Stunt Coordinator after a successful final stunt, hands in the air while everyone cheered, to give the footage to him as a gift later on. It never happened that way. I turned to "B" camera and made the motion to turn it off. I was not comfortable with us recording this man's death. It was the ultimate invasion of personal privacy. The back windshield blew open and access was gained to the body. But still, no response. We were deep in the middle of the Mojave Desert. The nearest hospital was an hour away by car. EMT had already called in Life Flight, though it would still be some time before they got there. Ten minutes felt like an hour. The first sign of life came from the sound recorder, who was signaling with thumbs up. Microphones inside the car had survived the impact and he was listening to the ordeal. It wasn't until a brace had been placed around the Stunt Coordinator's neck that the EMTs allowed him to walk out on his own. Then the clapping began. Life Flight turned around. The day was called off. No more shooting. The entire crew returned home and proceeded to get very, very drunk. After analyzing the crash, it was found that the Stunt Coordinator had missed his mark by a few inches. Instead of hitting in front of the right tire, he hit the chassis dead on. The still car did not crumble as it was supposed to, but acted like a brick wall as the moving car impacted against the solid area of the frame. As a result, neither car gave way and the Stunt Coordinator was knocked unconscious.

## The Lab and Transfer Facility

I have little to report in this area, as I was not invited to be a part of the film to tape transfer. What I do know was learned through the Director a few weeks after wrap. Apparently, some shots were severely over-exposed, past the point of salvage. On set, there were occasional times I metered incorrectly when using the polarizer for exterior shots. When using a polarizer, I apply a particular technique. Rather than compensating the standard two-stop light loss as they teach in film school, I spot meter through the filter at my desired angle of polarization. Unfortunately, I had just recently started using this technique and was not accustomed to it. If memory serves correct, I compensated for the standard two-stop light loss and metered through the filter. This caused me to believe the lens should be opened two more stops than it actually did, which resulted in an overexposed negative. I caught myself doing this intermittently throughout the shoot, but believed I had always realized in time to prevent any sort of mistake. It seems the unsalvageable images were the times I hadn't caught myself. As a result, I have learned to push harder for dailies, whether film or digital, even if they come only so often. Mistakes are always made and most can be realized in time to insure they don't happen again, unless they are never realized. Low-budget productions often claim they can't afford dailies; however, in my opinion, they can't afford not to. It always costs less to fix mistakes while shooting, as there may never be money for re-shoots and one time is the only time you'll have at each shot.

## The Day-to-Day

Shortly before shooting began, I signed onto a separate film in New York that started a day after wrapping the Barstow feature. Each evening, I carried on usual pre-production discussions late into the night with the other film's director. This balancing act between two productions required additional energy and time from the current job. It wasn't one of my best decisions, since hours of sleep were lost each night as a result. You will find yourself in a similar predicament time and again. Do take the back-to-back job offers when they come; however, be careful not to overextend yourself as the work and your reputation can ultimately suffer.

The few LA crewmembers and I checked out the film equipment and drove three hours to Barstow. We arrived at the hotel that became our home for the next several weeks and turned in for the night. The following morning, the film crew walked into Carrows diner chain to meet and greet for the first time. The obligatory first day speeches from key crewmembers complete, the Director rose to thank us for making his dreams come true and to inform that family members and ten of his credit cards were funding this film. The extent of financial risk he was taking did not go unnoticed. "If Robert Rodriguez can do it, then so can we!" Unfortunately, this didn't motivate all the crewmembers, including myself, having heard this speech many times before. Yet, something felt different with this Director and we readily admitted to our excitement. The meeting ended and those of us from out-of-town returned to the hotel. However, the Director had responsibilities at home with his wife and kids on the Marine base an hour away, and the Line Producer had decided to stay with him. This separation between crew proved to have a huge impact on our ability to plan for the following day's events throughout the shoot.

The excitement simmered down immediately after the first day began. The location was in the Director's house on the Marine base. It had been assumed the entry guards would let the film crew slip through without hassle. But on arrival we were detained at the security gate entrance for two hours filling out entrance paperwork.

As the day progressed, complications arose when balancing crew and acting responsibilities between the Barstow locals. To discuss the order of shots, I had to interrupt the AD rehearsing lines for the next scene. When a light needed to be set, the grip was found in the bathroom getting makeup done and the electric's role had been switched to boom man. Production had assumed little need for different people to fill the various roles, so assigned multiple responsibilities to each person. This tore people between duties, creating mass confusion and wasting precious time. The team worked hard, but the inexperienced locals moved painfully slow. The first shot got off four hours late. Any momentum created came to a complete halt when the Director attempted to perform the lead role of Zee. Each of his shots required three to four additional takes, as we coached him through directing and acting at the same time. By the end of day one, we had fallen drastically behind.

Day two proved far worse. It began with a dream sex scene between Zee and the lead actress, Laurie. Within minutes she stomped off set, refusing to take the action as far as the Director wished. The Director wasn't being disrespectful, but I understood

Laurie's frustration as the action had not been previously discussed or agreed upon. Despite his willingness to alter the scene, she refused to finish the day. Tempers flared between the two and the crew drove home another half day behind schedule. I knew we were in trouble for the long haul.

We woke up the following morning happy to be out of the cramped house on the Marine base. Having arrived at the desert location early, we were asked to wait in the travel van... for two hours. The morning quickly deteriorated into a series of fits from Laurie. Her make-up looked like shit. Her wardrobe looked too slutty. She was tired from the all the days we had worked (only two so far). Nothing made her happy. Fed up with the nonsense, the Director fired her on the spot and put her on a plane to who-cares-where. We didn't complete a single shot that day. Everyone returned to the hotel and a key crew meeting was called. The Director, AD, Line Producer, and I grouped in a circle of silence inside Room 18.

Director: I have to re-write the script.

Me: Okay. Can you get it done in the next few hours?

Director: No, I need more time than that.

Me: Why? You're only re-writing a scene or two.

Director: No, I mean the WHOLE script.

Me: Oh shit! You serious?

Director: Yeah, nothing is working. None of the scenes are right. I have to make it easier for me to play my role... give me less dialogue or something. I need to give Laurie less of a part because I don't know when I'll be able to get another one.

Me: That all makes sense. Should we move our first two days off to tomorrow and the next so you have that time to prepare?

Director: Yeah, that will be plenty of time. I'll be ready by then for sure.

Turning to the side, he began slashing all 110 pages with red ink. I walked the Line Producer and AD into the next room to discuss what we could do to better prepare the shooting days. I had noticed several standard set procedures were not being followed and began to rehash where we went wrong. My technical jargon and set lingo appeared to confuse them. Then it hit me. Shit! The Line Producer and AD had never performed these roles on a film set before either. Undiscouraged, I went back to the basics and taught them how to line a script, create a daily breakdown, and form lines of communication between the various departments. Every so often, the Director took a break from writing to learn how to create a shot list. He gave that to the AD and I showed him how to organize the shooting order. This ended our first day off. We had barely made headway. I wasn't sure the film would continue, thinking sometime tomorrow the Director might call the whole thing off.

I was extremely disappointed about the situation, but wanted nothing more than to trudge on and hope for the best. However, previous experience had taught me to protect my crew's interests, with that past production audited by the IRS fresh in my memory. I called a meeting with the Director and his sole confidant, the Line Producer, to relate my concerns about our ability to finish the film. "The crew is still here and wants to give 100% for you, but before that happens we need to have our agreed sum of payment up front," I told them. Without hesitation, the Director agreed and began making phone calls to his bank. My request was not ordinary, nor is it something I have done since. Because we were already getting paid so little and Production was bleeding money to solve problems, I was scared the crew might be left hanging in the wind when the money ran out. Little did I know this single power play on my part would dramatically affect the relationship between the Director and myself.

We resumed preparation the following day. A new actress was plucked from the local theatre troupe for the role of Laurie. The Director made good headway on the script. The crew lay by the pool drinking and taking the occasional dip in the cool water. Everyone was in good spirits.

(*Hotel door busts open*)

Director: I found a new actor for Zee!

Me: I thought you were going to do it?

Director: I'm no good and I can't concentrate on directing. I talked to one of the stunt guys and he really wants to do it. The script isn't working either; let's go back to the old script. We can make it work now.

The AD, Line Producer and I scrambled to re-organize the shoot according to the old script. Because roles had been recast, we needed to re-shoot the first two days at the Marine base. Instead of having 18 days to shoot 110 pages, we now had 16 days. Motivation ran high, and to everyone's credit, not a single person lost their patience. The Director did everything possible to make things work. The day ended once we agreed which scenes could be cut if time ran out. The Director and Line Producer drove back to his house well after sunset.

Those two days off were the last nights anyone slept peacefully. When shooting resumed, my routine every morning began at four o'clock with an hour phone call to the director of the production in New York. Then I knocked on each crewmember's door to wake them. Made sure everything and everyone was loaded in the cars and headed off to wherever set was that day, always arriving on time. Organizational tasks such as assembling the crew, loading equipment, and printing travel directions every morning is not the responsibility of the cinematographer. I inadvertently took the responsibility but quickly became fed up with Production's lack of recognition for the burden I had shouldered.

Filming began with a fresh start. I had high hopes... again. But the two days of planning had changed very little. We bogged down in miscommunication and lack of organization. Like the first two days, our problems were a direct result of crewmembers acting in the film. The actor replacing the Director in the role of Zee was in fact a man from the stunt team who had always wanted to be cast in a lead role. In truth, he had no acting experience and was cast because he was the only guy the Director knew that had a dark skin-tone.

Despite all these troubles, the decision to shoot in July ultimately became the movie's undoing. The Director asked his wife to perform the daily catering in a desire to save money on the food budget. She was on maternity leave from the Marine base during this time. Her due date was close at hand however, and she was too physically exhausted to cook. This created constant friction at home, which affected his work ethic on set. Not surprisingly, a heat wave hit California during the month and we found ourselves working in 125° F heat. I drank so much water each day that my stomach would cramp up. The average workday lasted fourteen hours. The crew worked to exhaustion, which quickly became a health issue. Regardless, Production demanded more to make up for the short shooting schedule. One particular afternoon we shot a scene in a junkyard. The sun radiated off the sand, reflecting even hotter off the metal cars. Near the end of the long day, the Director asked for a few more takes. The crew eagerly agreed, not wanting to endure this location hell again for any pickup shots. An hour and a half later we were still shooting. Again, the Director asked for more time. I turned my head to look at the crew; a few had heat stroke, one was delirious, and another spoke incoherently. I called an end to our work and told the Director I couldn't ask any more from the crew that day. Sixteen hours had passed under the oppressive heat. He pulled me aside, demanding to know why I wouldn't let him keep shooting his movie.

Me: First off, it's not your movie, it's all of ours. We want to finish this as badly as you do.

Director: But you can't tell me when we stop shooting. Do you know how much of my own money I've put into this?

Me: Yeah, about ten credit cards worth; you've made that clear several times. But you have to consider the crew. Right now they are here working. But if they keep getting abused like this, they may not be here tomorrow. Then it won't matter how many cards you've spent.

Our relationship became a strange dichotomy after that. We worked well together as a director and cinematographer, but when I had to put on the AD's or Line Producer's hat (remember, those two were busy acting), we constantly butted heads. The multiple roles on a film set naturally create a system of checks and balances. This allows for accountability to be spread out evenly. Though the director is the captain of the ship, others do hold equal shares of power in their positions. An AD will decide when to move on to the next shot in the interest of completing the day's schedule. An LP will dictate whether production can allow the crew to work overtime in the interest of budgetary constraints. The director is included in these decisions but ultimately it is out of his or her hands. If a single person becomes responsible for governing every situation, this can lead to frustrations becoming focused solely on that individual. Because I began to partially fill each of these roles, I was unable to improve our working relationship, often coming off as the "bad guy" that limited the Director's artistic vision. This culminated in the final week, after laying down a defining ultimatum that permanently affected our relationship. Throughout the shoot, I had roused the troops each morning and drove them to set on time. Yet the Director and Line Producer arrived late each day. He was having difficulty juggling between the shoot and caring for his pregnant wife and two little girls. I was sympathetic to the situation from the beginning, but as the weeks passed by, they continued to arrive each day one to two hours late. He assumed the twelve-hour shooting day didn't officially start until they were there.

Me: You are late again. This is the last time.

Director: What do you mean?

Me: I'm not going to allow the crew to work over 12 hours any more. You two have lost that privilege.

Director: But we've only been shooting for 12 hours every day, no more.

Me: Yes, but that is actual shooting hours. The crew is here for an hour or two prepping while you two show up late every morning and then also wrapping for an hour after that. Until you show respect to the crew by arriving on time, then I will only allow them to work for the standard twelve hours, which starts at the call time.

Director: But the crew knew we were going to work every day for 14 to 16 hours. This is a low-budget film. I warned you and you said that would be all right.

Me: You are right. I did. But that doesn't mean you can show up late. A director, especially when directing a low-budget film, needs to be here at all times to lead the crew by example. The crew is getting paid very little if at all for their work; they're here because they believe in the film and want to be part of something special. All you have to do is show up on time and everything will be okay. How hard is that? Set your alarm clock earlier for Christ's sake. Do what you have to do, just lead by example.

He agreed to this, but repeatedly showed up late. As a result, I continued to call an end to the day's shooting at twelve hours after call time. He yelled and hollered, but I had to stand firm. The intense July heat wave was exhausting the crew and it became dangerous working with the stunts. Being tired increased the likelihood of accidents happening. As a cinematographer, your first responsibility, above all else, is the safety of the crew. Never bend to the pressure of any production. No film is ever worth a person's life.

## Mishaps and the Unexpected

As if on-set politics weren't enough, plenty of mishaps occurred along the way. Though painful at the time, they are somewhat amusing to look back on.

When shooting in the desert, obvious local wildlife to be wary of include snakes, scorpions... and bees? I had no idea bees even existed in the dry desert. On the hottest day, they swarmed from their holes, seeking the only moisture available: our bodies. To keep cool, the crew wrapped their heads and shoulders in water-soaked towels or handkerchiefs. Throughout the day, a person's head would be swallowed by an enormous pack of these insects trying to drink the water. Only two crewmembers escaped without a sting that day, myself being one. Everyone else was stung several times, the 1ˢᵗ AC getting the brunt of it when he received one strike to his left nut. This prompted the crew to immediately tape their shorts and sleeves closed, making it even hotter as this prevented air circulation. The 1ˢᵗ AC went to the doctor the following day after his legs began to swell.

One particular stunt scene involved a gunfight foot chase along the streets of Barstow. The neighborhood locations appeared perfect and the crew was set to go. We were going to drive around, screeching tires and shooting everything from handguns to shotguns. In short, make a lot of noise. Standard set procedure for this activity is to hire town police to protect the set and act as a voice of authority. The night before, a stunt man warned us of local headlines regarding our chosen neighborhood locations. There had been a rise in gang activity and several shootings had occurred over the last month in that area. The next morning came, only to find no police officers had been hired. Instead of running in fear of gunshots, the locals seemed more than likely to stop by for some fun, bringing their own guns to our party. No one seemed to give it much thought, but I was considerably scared all day and thankful when it ended with everyone safe. Well, not entirely everyone. At one point we were capturing a running sequence from the back of a flatbed truck. Red was to keep his running speed alongside us. This forced him to flat out sprint around corners and over curbs. One such take sent Red tumbling onto the pavement, damaging his knee. He finished filming that day and tried to do most of his actions for the rest of the shoot, but pain showed on his face when pushed too far. After returning to LA, an MRI showed he had torn muscles in his knee.

The hotel we were staying in turned out to be a former crack den turned halfway house for convicts. Exhausted every night, we usually fell asleep at the flick of a light switch. This fatigue was indirectly to our benefit, as sundown signaled the surfacing of hotel misfits. They broke through windows, tore holes in the walls, and threw rocks at our rental equipment truck. Drinking, yelling, fighting, this place had it all. After the first night, the Gaffer and I woke up in our room and noticed it smelled like cat piss and cigarettes. It was listed as a non-smoking room and had been cleaned of cat hair, so I assumed the carpet was old and had soaked up those smells over time. I went to the front desk to ask the owner for a new room.

Owner: But that is our finest room. We re-modeled it a few days ago.

Me: Maybe, but it smells like cat urine and cigarettes.

Owner: I was in there just yesterday and it smelled fine. Maybe it's the cleaning solution used for the bathroom.

Me: Ma'am, if it is, then maybe it's not cleaning so well and you should use another brand.

Owner: The senator of California comes to Barstow and when he does, he always stays here in that room. He was just here a few weeks ago. It's his favorite room.

Me: Ma'am, if the Senator of California is staying in this room when he comes to visit Barstow, I'm sure he doesn't keep coming here for the sleep.

Owner: If you don't like it, then go find another hotel. I have no other rooms for you.

Which wasn't true, but I had obviously insulted her and the pride she took in the hotel and its newly-renovated state. We learned the hotel recently caught fire from overheated electrical wiring and she had just finished repairs. One night, a huge blaze started in a hotel two buildings away from us. It took five hours to extinguish the flames. The cause was another electrical fire from the desert heat. Apparently this is common for old electrical systems and happens all the time in Barstow. It seemed it would only be a matter of time before my belongings burned while I was away at work, or perhaps I woke with a fire blazing around my head.

## The Big Finale

Amazingly enough, we completed filming the entire script minus one deleted sub-plot. The work totaled 100 pages in 16 days, including a week and a half of stunt work. Fucking incredible.

The day after wrap, I flew to New York and began prep on the other film. Over the following month I called the Director periodically, curious to know how the dailies looked. No response. He never answered his phone and no matter how many messages I left with his wife, he never called back. I contacted the post facility, but per a confidentiality agreement they signed...

Post Facility: We can't speak about the footage without the Director's permission.

Me: I'm Austin Schmidt, I should be allowed to see it.

Post Facility: Uh huh... and you are?

Me: I'm the cinematographer who shot the film!

Post Facility: Oh... right... but we still need his permission.

I feared something was terribly wrong at that point and thought perhaps he had retained some of his frustrations from the shoot. When we eventually connected, he relayed that some shots were overexposed and beyond saving, but still wouldn't allow me to see the footage. "Not until I'm ready for you to see it," he said. Over several phone calls, he relayed his anger with my actions on set and the disrespect he felt from everybody. I stated my argument and explained why events unfolded the way they had. By the end of these difficult conversations, we appeared to be in a good place and a promise was made to review the footage together once the first cut was complete. We also decided that pick-ups of several scenes were in order, which would be done the following summer.

Months later his number appeared on my cell phone, asking to meet at the coffee shop where we first met. Usually it takes thirty minutes, but traffic was horrible and the drive took an hour. It didn't matter, I was bubbling with excitement. I hadn't seen a single frame of film, until that day. When I walked into the coffee shop, I noticed the Line Producer there, for moral support maybe, but why? The second thing I noticed was an absence of any computer to watch footage on. I knew then what was about to happen. Courtesy handshakes and hellos were exchanged. We sat down.

Director: I'm going to cut to the chase. We have decided your services are no longer needed for the pick-ups.

(*A smile from me and a nod of the head; how else could I react?*)

Director: We feel the scenes that need to be shot, I can do myself. You will still get deferred pay, points, and credit as the cinematographer. I would also like you to be a part of the final color correction when that time comes, but you will not be needed for anything else.

(*He had just gotten his audiotapes back a month ago and had listened to them for the first time. The sound recorder rolled well before and after every take. A few choice conversations were heard that renewed bad memories.*)

Director: It just brought me back to how frustrated I was with you. I felt everyone was rude and disrespectful.

*(I know I said a few things that weren't necessary or helpful to the situation at hand and wished I had dealt with them differently.)*

Director: I also can't believe you demanded all your money at the beginning of the shoot. I had no way to insure you guys would stay on the job. I don't want to deal with that stress again.

*(Which was the point in demanding our money in the first place. Once Production proved their lack of organization and inexperience I wasn't about to give them leverage over us.)*

Director: Do you have anything you want to say?

*(What did he expect from me? To get mad, scream and defend myself? What good would that do?)*

Me: Well, you and I have talked a lot about this over the phone for some time. I don't see any point in explaining again. You obviously feel the way you feel, and no amount of words from me is going to change that.

Director: You're right. Let's leave it at that. Thank you, though. This experience was like film school for me. I would have spent as much going to film school, but instead completed a feature and gained real-world experience. I have you to thank for a big part of that.

Line Producer: Yeah, I learned so much too.

Me: Glad I could help you with that.

We parted ways after a half-hour of discussion and I began the long drive home in traffic to Marina del Rey. I doubted I would ever see a frame of footage.

## Reflections

I felt betrayed after the Director's decision over the next year. It created a well of resentment after all the hard work I put in. Not many people would have persevered through the hardship and responsibility like I had. It hurt the most that the Director saw my efforts in a completely opposite light.

I continued shooting films after that but came to the point where I didn't like being a cinematographer, only working to pay off debts accumulated while getting to this point in my career. The bitterness from that experience trickled down into work and ultimately, into life. I hated hearing of another person's success. They couldn't deserve it more than me. I had put in my time. I shouldn't have to scratch as much as I still do. I blamed my misery and frustration on everything around me, but never myself.

By this time, I had a sizeable chunk of money put away; as I had learned over the years, when you're up it's only a matter of time before you're down again. Always have money tucked away for the times work is scarce. Problem was, this particular time lasted four months. I didn't mind it at first, until the money started coming to its end. Credit cards were maxed. I couldn't get any loans. My parents were unable to financially assist me. It seemed I would have to sell my camera package. It was during this time of financial desperation when I remembered why I fell in love with cinematography in the first place. My perspective of the occupation changed direction, and I became at peace with the situation. It would all work out. How I didn't know, but it would all work out. I thought back on events surrounding the feature and realized I hadn't applied any of what I had learned; making the whole experience a complete waste.

Looking back, I had wanted to lay blame on Production for the shortcomings of the film and all the troubles we had. I realized I was equally responsible for the mishaps. We as cinematographers are accountable for what happens during a production. It is our responsibility to share knowledge and protect a production with our wisdom to the best of our ability. This will make a happier and more positive atmosphere, which in turn improves the process of making the film. While in pre-production, I should have addressed the cautionary red flags I had avoided in the early excitement of shooting my first feature film. I had ignored my intuition and everyone paid dearly for it. Addressing red flags may result in difficult conversations and uncomfortable moments, but it is best to confront these issues early on when they are still solvable. Stay strong and confident in your resolve. Do not blindly assume that everything will just work out in the end as I did. This leaves too much room for the unknown. You may not comprehend these words, as it will take your own personal experience to fully grasp what I am saying. But I promise, there will be that single moment when it all clicks together, allowing you to enjoy every aspect of this wonderful occupation for the rest of your life.

Never forget the passion of your youth. There is no right or wrong way to go about it. Utilize your natural instincts, business savvy and a little bullshit from time to time. But always remember: be careful of what you say while on set. You never know when audio is rolling.

VLF
Film

407 823 1355

Made in the USA
Charleston, SC
15 October 2011